Dhamma Moments

Danai Chanchaochai

Dhamma Moments

CO-PUBLISHERS Post Books, The Post Publishing Plc.

136 Na Ranong Road, off Sunthornkosa Road,
Klong Toey, Bangkok 10110, Thailand
Tel: 0-2240-3700 ext. 1691-2 Fax: 0-2671-9698
email: postbooks@bangkokpost.co.th
www.bangkokpost.com/postbooks

DMG Books, Direct Media Group (Thailand) Co., Ltd.
11th Floor, Tonson Tower, 900 Ploenchit Road,
Patumwan, Bangkok 10330, Thailand
Tel: 0-2658-6433 Fax: 0-2658-6448-9

© Danai Chanchaochai 2003

EDITORS Kelvin Rugg, Denis Segaller
FIRST PUBLISHED 2003
PRINTER Allied Printers, The Post Publishing Plc.
SET IN Gil Sans 1 & Univers

NATIONAL LIBRARY OF THAILAND CATALOGING-IN-PUBLICATION DATA
Danai Chanchaochai
    Dhamma Moments. -- Bangkok :
    Post Books & Direct Media Group,   2003. 240 p.
    1. Dhamma. 1. Title. 294.3144

ISBN 974-91347-4-5

Contents

Dhamma moments in daily life

FOREWORD

A most elegant characteristic of Buddhist teachings is that they can be practised at varying levels and to varying extents as chosen and deemed appropriate at the time by a person. Nobody can, or should try to, reach *Nirvana* in one swoop—it would be just too big a stretch for any human. Management of life is an ongoing process, which by Buddhist definition of the universe, will continue life after life until enlightenment—a conscious state of permanent peace—is ultimately achieved. That can take a while. And it will require work and perseverance. In the meantime, one must get going step by step. In life, everyone must make the best of the hand each has been dealt. Notwithstanding a belief in the Law of *Karma*, central to Buddhist teachings, one must not just let life pass on listlessly but rather attempt to continuously improve oneself in a correct way—for in the final analysis, one is the master of one's destiny. No power from any divine beings—even though Buddhism does not deny the existence of such—can substitute for one's own deeds and determination to effectively solve one's life problems. Self-reliance to attain the wisdom to see and do the right things—and there are guidelines for going about this—is much preached by the Lord Buddha as opposed to just praying for salvation. Regardless of how arduous the task and the journey, one must ensure that one is moving in an upward spiral of spiritual improvement that makes for quality life along the way, and ultimately reaches the end of suffering.

It is easy to preach compassion, control, forgiveness and many other kinds of virtue. But in real life, given the constant pressure of trying to make a living, of having to start with some deficiencies, of encountering injustices, one would naturally find it difficult to stay true to a recommended course of spiritual improvement. That is why a strong will and a lot of hard work are absolute requisites for not dropping out from such a path. Well-intended writings, like *Dhamma Moments* and many others, can be helpful. *Dhamma Moments*, in particular, attempts to bring to light the Buddhist teachings in an understandable and identifiable way within the context of everyday modern life, and the trappings of materialism. But in the end, each person gets out of Buddhism what he puts into practising its "guidelines" day in day out—not just at the temples, or in the prayer room in one's house, but at every moment of consciousness. I wish us all, as co-passengers in a journey through seemingly endless cycles of births, deaths, and all the suffering in between, steady progress according to Lord Buddha's *Dhamma*—and eventual attainment of permanent peace.

Banthoon Lamsam
President & CEO
Kasikornbank Plc

FOREWORD

Stress and strife in our contemporary world are increasingly turning the minds of many people to the values and lessons of religion. Buddhism is a particularly strong refuge given the purity and simplicity of its message. *Dhamma Moments* by Danai Chanchaochai is an extremely valuable and relevant contribution in this context. The author brings into relief the distilled wisdom of Buddha's teachings and offers some real life examples of the impact of the Dhamma on people around us. *Dhamma Moments* is a book to read and re-read and treasured.

Jennie Chua
Chairman & CEO
Raffles International Ltd

FOREWORD

Danai Chanchaochai started his weekly column, "Dhamma Moments", in the *Bangkok Post*'s Real.Time section in August 2002. In it he explores everyday social karma with a keen insight into our civil microcosm. A simple guide that advocates a different approach. His writing provides a refreshing perception that makes us pause and think what and who we are in the social labyrinth of society.

In the chaos of modern city life, we assume others should practise the common courtesies that we ourselves often overlook. We rush though our daily routine with such frightening monotony that we tend to fall victim to our own bad habits without realising it. We make snap judgements of others, carelessly ignoring our own karma. Our moral actions greatly affect our lives and the lives of others.

Everyone can benefit from a little clarity. Many people search for focus through meditation, eager to retune senses dulled with images of happiness, success and riches from countless television and radio images. Our perceptions have become obscured and tainted with each new advertising campaign. We frequently forget that the path to self-realisation and ultimate peace lies within us.

Dhamma Moments provides a tangible reference to a "better self". The dialogues are realistic scenarios to which everyone can relate. The lessons learned are easy to understand. The advice is gentle. The passages are concise and elegant.

This book is a compilation of Danai's perceptions translated into subtly worded articles, in which he makes many delightful observations. Danai uses simple approaches to put forward key ideas, be they personal such as self-image, social as in common courtesy or the psyche of first impression. His insights into social customs and morals are truly inspirational. His gentle style stimulates our consciousness and stirs quiet moments of reflection.

It is hard to get good and free advice nowadays. Friends are sometimes biased out of loyalty. Parents don't always understand the problems. *Dhamma Moments* offers sound, non-biased advice for people of all ages and for all occasions.

Prapai Kraisornkovit
Editor, Real.Time
Bangkok Post

Dhamma teachings

The great awakening

**The Lord Buddha's teachings
help us to create
a sense of perspective**

One of the many stories about the Buddha tells of how soon after his Enlightenment he happened upon a man along the road who was struck by the Buddha's extraordinary radiance and peaceful presence. The man stopped and asked, "My friend, what are you? Are you a celestial being or a god?"

"I am neither," said the Buddha.

"Well, then, are you a magician or a wizard?"

"No," replied the Buddha.

"Then what are you?"

"I am awake," said the Buddha.

Can we say the same thing about ourselves? Are we truly awake, really mindful of the world in which we live, fully aware of all its temptations on the one hand and the enormous potential for good it offers on the other?

Being unaware of even the physical world around us seems to be an increasing phenomenon in what is today's consumer-oriented world. We often tend to encounter people so wrapped up with their own affairs that they will, for instance, pause to hold a family conversation at the foot of a busy escalator or stop to window-shop on a narrow pavement, apparently unconcerned or unaware that others are being inconvenienced by their actions.

Certainly, they can't claim to be awake. That type of unawareness may seem trivial, the action of individuals so preoccupied with their own affairs that they are unmindful of their surroundings or the presence of other people. It is however symptomaic of a situation in which we can all find ourselves when we lose sight of the need to be mindful of every moment.

This of course is where the Buddha's teachings can be so helpful. They offer sound practical advice on staying aware of the world in which we live, of being awake.

Let's look at some of the ways this advice can help to change our lives, to give them the purpose so many of us seek, yet fail to achieve.

First of all, Buddism's focus on attentiveness and mindfulness is a wonderful antidote to denial. Our first line of defence in dealing with difficult issues, denial can have devastating effects.

Denial of an addiction, denial of a relationship problem, denial of personal shortcomings, denial even of death—it is a demon with many forms. As in overcoming fear, we must first of all accept its existence—we must not deny denial itself. When we can do that, we have taken the first step in overcoming whatever problem we have been trying to avoid. Being mindful and aware, being really awake, does more than break down the doors of denial. It also keeps us focused on the present. And if we are focused on this moment, we won't be dwelling on the past. We won't be in the land of guilt, regret and revenge. Nor will we be thinking pointlessly about the future—a land of uncertainty. The present moment, with all its potential for beauty and opportunity, is a much better place to dwell, and the only place we can ever really BE.

Another great example of how Buddhism can be helpful in our everyday life is the way it helps us create a sense of perspective. The belief, for instance, that there is no self, helps put into perspective our significance in the greater scheme of things. It helps us realise that this world and whatever is beyond can get on very well with or without us, that we are in fact such little things when the stars come out. And knowing this certainly puts things in perspective, reminding us that we really don't need to take ourselves or life in general too seriously. There is in fact a good reason for that big Buddhist smile.

One of the basic human challenges is learning to let go. Here again Buddhism comes to the rescue. Almost daily in some way or other we are called on to let go. To let go of our children as they mature, of spells of anger, resentment and hurt. We are called to let go of our own self-identity as we evolve and move through the stages of life. We have to let go of memories both good and bad, and accept that change and impermanence are part of our lives.

Buddhism also remind us that the opposite of letting go—craving, grasping, clinging—leads inevitably to disappointment and unhappiness. Even when what we desire is a good thing such as love, for instance, we must accept that it won't last forever, unchanged, contrary to the words of many popular songs.

But perhaps the most important thing that Buddhism can teach us is the art of living according to the Middle Path, of living life to the full without attachment, seizing each moment, keeping in step with its eternal rhythm.

This, after all, is how the Buddha himself lived. After he attained Enlightenment he remained fully engaged—with his community, his neighbours, his followers, with the world around him.

But he was attached to none of it, not even to life itself. This is the secret of living a Buddhist life.

Cultivating awareness, of mindfulness, through meditation is without doubt one of the most effective ways of mastering that secret. It's effective because by applying ourselves conscientiously and diligently to its practice, meditation will help us let go.

It's all in the mind

We can all learn from the story of the fantastic
but troubled mathematician John Nash,
even though we may never attain his brilliance

Only now are scientists begin-
ning to fully appreciate the power of the mind. In medicine,
for example, they witness its incredible healing power.
They accept this power as a very special, intangible force,
yet they still do not understand fully what it is, or how
it works.

Perhaps first we should ask ourselves what we mean
when we refer to our mind. "It's all in the mind," we say.
But where is the mind? Our brain helps us use our mind
on a physical level, but we know that our brain and our
mind are not one and the same. "By the mind of man we

understand that in him which thinks, remembers, reasons, wills," is one such definition. "The intellectual or rational faculty in man; the understanding; the intellect; the power that conceives, judges, or reasons; also, the entire spiritual nature; the soul," is another.

However we define the mind, we all know that it is our mind that defines us. It determines who we are and what we are. A core Buddhist belief says, "Mind is the master. With the mind everything is possible." The Thai saying, "Mind is the master, body is the slave," reminds us of this basic wisdom.

How then can we use the infinite power of our minds to lead a richer, more meaningful life? We can learn much to help us from the discourses of the Buddha. "I know not of any other single thing so intractable as the untamed mind. The untamed mind is indeed a thing intractable," said the Buddha. But this is followed by: "I know not of any other single thing so tractable as the tamed mind. The tamed mind is indeed a thing tractable."

Speaking to an audience of monks, the Buddha continued, "I know not of any single thing that brings such woe as the mind that is untamed, uncontrolled, unguarded, and unrestrained. Such a mind indeed brings great woe." But then he said, "I know not of any single thing that brings such bliss as the mind that is tamed, controlled, guarded, and restrained. Such a mind indeed brings great bliss."

The film *A Beautiful Mind*, in which Russell Crowe gave an impressive performance, is based on the true story of John Nash, a brilliant American mathematician, who was the recipient of the 1994 Nobel Prize for Economics. His ground-breaking proposition, the Nash Equilibrium, changed aspects of economic theory that had been taught for centuries. Given his accomplishments, it's hard to believe he struggled with schizophrenia.

He had his own unique way of dealing with the world, explaining natural phenomena with his unusual grasp of mathematics. Refusing to attend school, he lived instead in a world he created for himself in his mind. He became increasingly delusional and the film shows how, with the help of his wife and psychiatric counselling, he finally gained control of his brilliant mind.

We can all learn from the story of John Nash even though we may never attain his brilliance. The lesson is clear enough. As the Thai saying goes, "The mind may be the master of the body," but we must learn also to follow the wisdom of the Buddha: "I know not of any other single thing so tractable as the tamed mind", and become master of our mind.

We are, after all, what we think we are. We often talk about wishing to have peace of mind, as if it is something others can bestow on us, when in fact it can come only from within ourselves. As we begin that process of introspection we can learn much from these wise words:

"Watch your thoughts: they become words
Watch your words; they become actions
Watch your actions; they become habits
Watch your habits; they become your character
Watch your character; it becomes your destiny"

Frank Outlaw

Life's simple beauties

Just as rice and curry complement each other,
so mind and body must function together

The way of life for many Thai people has changed dramatically over recent years. Today, more than ever, we seem to be competing with time. "I simply don't have time" is a common expression. Busy schedules, simply getting to our place of work at the appointed time, allow us little space for ourselves—that private and personal space when we can take stock of where we are going with our lives, and how we plan to get there.

Many Thais will remember that when they were young they often went to a temple with their parents or grandparents. And they brought rice and curry to offer to the monks. This was a great moment in their young lives, they did it with a pure heart and with respect for the monks, who pass on the Buddha's teachings for us in this life.

Food for monks traditionally includes rice and curry. You wouldn't eat either by itself; they go together, they complement one another. Our mind and the vehicle we occupy in this life—our body—must also function together, for us to be a complete person, healthy both in body and mind.

Keeping our mind and body together is not always easy. Sometimes when we are engaged in an everyday task, for instance, our mind wanders, it becomes unfocussed and unguarded, thereby allowing unwanted and unhealthy thoughts of temptation and desire to slip in and take over.

The lesson here is clear enough: we should always be mindful. Without mindfulness, even the simplest task in life can become full of difficulties. But with mindfulness, when we are truly focussed, we can see that even a simple task has a purpose, and because of what it can show us, it also has a beauty of its own.

Continuing on the theme of what we eat, the Buddha warned us not to pay attention to the trimmings, the tempting desserts that we really don't need. In some cultures mothers tell their children, "If you don't eat your meat and vegetables, you won't get any dessert."

Mothers of course know that meat and vegetables, rice and curry are the most nutritious part of the meal, and all that is necessary for the child. They also recognise that temptation, the promise of a favourite dessert, is a powerful incentive for the child to first eat what's good for it.

As adults, when we are mindful, we'll find that rice and curry are enough for each meal. We will no longer crave the dessert. We will find that maintaining a constant harmony of our body and mind, a balance between what our body needs and what our mind desires, will give us the ability to live this life with a sense of contentment.

That contentment, and the sense of fulfilment it brings, comes from within ourselves, we no longer need the short-lived pleasures of life's desserts, pleasures that always have their price.

Without their temptation, we will continue to develop as a well-rounded human being. We become more and more capable of finding contentment within our own mind and through our own wisdom. We no longer need to look for external happiness, and as we develop, our social and physical freedom will be preserved and strengthened.

Think of a mother and a demanding child. While walking down the street, they pass by a toyshop which displays a very expensive toy. The mother hasn't much money to spare, but the child drags her, as children do, into the shop. That toy is the most important thing in the child's life at that moment, and finally, perhaps for the sake of peace and quiet, the mother gives in and buys the toy she can ill afford.

The next day that toy is in pieces, discarded by the child as something of no more interest. The pleasure it brought was transitory, but the hardship it would cause, the strain on the family budget, would be long-lasting.

As adults we generally put aside childish things, but we can still be distracted by temptations when our mind and body are not in harmony. Maintaining mindfulness, being aware of the moment, will help us resist the temptation of life's desserts. When we follow the teachings of the Buddha we will know that rice and curry are enough in themselves, and that they should always accompany each other.

Breaking the cycle

Gain freedom from the bonds of craving
by being mindful and compassionate

In the *Bangkok Post*'s Outlook
section of August 25, 2002, a very well written account
looked at the life and work of painter Amnart Klanparacha.
Appropriately entitled "The Art of Living", the feature
provided an insightful view of the artist and the man. We
learnt that for him at least, art is about practising mindfulness. Not surprisingly he believes that his art should
convey the essence of life, nature and Dhamma.

He also described how he has struggled to understand
the Buddhist concept of *Paticca Samuppada*—the law of

the Cycle of Dependent Origination which, in fact, is the theme of his latest series of works.

We may not all be blessed with the creative talent that allows artists such as Amnart to express the truths of his Buddhist beliefs so visually, but each one of us possesses an ability to express ourselves in our own way. We can do it with a kind act, an encouraging smile or simply by a right thought.

Amnart's attempt to understand a complicated aspect of Buddhism such as Paticca Samuppada is in itself a liberating and enlightening experience. He has already opened his mind to the joy of discovery in the never-ending process of self-examination, of questioning, that is the essence of existence of all beings, of life itself. "Day and night, I carefully observed what was happening in my mind, in order to see if what the Buddha said is true, and how true it is," Amnart was reported as saying.

Paticca Samuppada—the law of the Cycle of Dependent Origination—is certainly too complex to be addressed fully in *Dhamma Moments*, but it can be summarised as being an analysis of existence in terms of cause and effect. There are twelve links to this, forming a circle. The starting point is ignorance which leads to the following in turn: volition, consciousness, mental and physical existence, sense organs, sense impressions, feeling, craving, clinging, process of existence, rebirth, decay and death. To destroy craving (*tanha*), therefore, is to break the circle.

This fundamental concept questions what "life" or "existence" is. For most people, the answer is delusion and karma-formations (activities that stem from delusion). Our delusions keep us always active, always making new karma. Consciousness means being aware of something. It is consciousness which brings into effect the interplay of mind and matter, which is existence. We spend our time seeing and enjoying visual forms, hearing and enjoying sounds, smelling and enjoying scents, tasting and enjoying flavours, touching and enjoying bodily feelings, thinking and fantasising and enjoying thoughts, imaginings, daydreams.

From the time we wake up until we fall asleep at night, we spend our time looking, listening, smelling, tasting, feeling, or being lost in thoughts and fantasies. There is no rest at all from these activities. How then can we escape from this cycle of karma, cause and effect?

If we don't abandon our sense of self-identity, we are bound to suffer pain and alienation, as our "self" inevitably falls subject to circumstances outside our control. To gain freedom from this predicament, we must first develop a healthy sense of self, based on being mindful and compassionate, both to ourselves and to others. Then we must learn how to be at one with the present moment—which by definition is always changing but is always "now". Observing the present, we see that our "self" is quite simply an internal collection of desires, memories and imaginings. We then must learn to transcend this craving aspect of our "self" and seek liberation from the shackle it imposes on our lives.

Amnart talks of his own quest to find an answer, and describes how, when in his 20s, he set off on a 10-year journey of living the ascetic life of a wanderer, staying at temples, in the forest, even in a cemetery and a disused tiger's den. Does this mean we should all wander in the forests, living the life of a recluse, in search of our own truth?

If we have the time, and the inclination, we could do just that. But we can also do it without moving a muscle. Through *Vipassana* meditation we can wander into the forests of delusion, of lust and passion, of craving and clinging. We can learn how to find the path through the dense foliage to the sunlit clearing where we will see clearly the truth of *dukkha*, that existence is suffering and misery, and that craving (tanha) is the cause of all suffering.

It is then for us to plant our own flowers in the forest.

A universal message

People the world over can embrace
Buddhism's ideals and
benefit from its wisdom

I recently had occasion to take
a trip with a small group of friends to Udon Thani, and the
opportunity to visit Wat Pa Baan Taad. Mingling with the
early morning crowds outside this well known temple,
I was struck by the timeless quality of the image of the
long line of monks winding their way to the hundreds of
waiting almsgivers.

As they came closer I noticed several farang faces
among the monks. And seeing them, clearly at ease with
their fellows, composed and self effacing, I had a sense
of quiet elation. Here the spirit of Dhamma seemed to

hang in the very air. I felt privileged to be part of that special Dhamma moment as I was reminded of the universal nature of the Buddha's message.

Although many Thai people may have travelled to other countries, perhaps studying and working abroad for extended periods, most will probably spend their lives here. Their opinions and attitudes will be shaped by their own cultural and social mores, and because of Buddhism's traditional influence on the national psyche, they may see the Buddha's teachings from a narrow and even nationalistic perspective.

After the chanting and a spirited interview session with the still feisty Venerable Maha Boowa Nanasampanno, an encounter with a young British couple further reminded me that the very real benefits to be derived from following Buddhist teachings are available to everyone, and that people the world over can embrace Buddhism's ideals and benefit from its wisdom.

Julie was here with her husband on holiday, and as she said, "to simply experience a land where Dhamma is part of the fabric of society." I took that as a compliment, and although I wondered if it were really so, I was impressed by her obvious sincerity and quiet conviction.

It was clear that Julie wanted to share her experiences, and soon, with some occasional prompting from her husband, she explained how she first became interested in Vipassana meditation and how, later it would have a profound effect on her life.

"So how did it all begin?" I asked. Eager to tell her story, Julie explained, "Well, I first went to some meditation classes back in our home town, but the timing was inconvenient, it clashed with my weekly cooking class and I stopped going for a while. Then some new classes started up just a short drive from our house, and in a way it really all began from there."

"And did you find them helpful?" "Yes, very. The classes had a good, supportive atmosphere, very friendly and relaxed. The meditation helped a lot. It made my mind more peaceful for maybe two or three days after the class. But it was a while before I realised that if I meditated every day I could feel peaceful every day! I began to bring a bit more wisdom into my life."

"Do you think your life has changed much since you began learning about Buddhist meditation?" "It was a gradual change. At first it was only small things, such as becoming a bit more patient and a bit more tolerant. But

I think I realised quite quickly that it was what I'd been looking for."

"How do you mean?"

"I wasn't consciously looking for a religion, but I definitely had a feeling of needing some inner strength."

"Inner strength?"

"Yes. At that time my parents were both getting old, and I knew that my father had heart disease and was going to die quite soon. So it was partly worry about how I would be able to cope with his death and support my mother and family that first brought me to the classes."

"What about your family, do you think they were helped as well?"

"Certainly it helped them a lot over the next couple of years. It helped me to work on improving my relationships with my family. It was about two and a half years later that my father died, and by that time I felt I had developed a great deal of strength and could offer a lot of support to my family, especially my mother. I understood that my and my family's sufferings were the result of being in *samsara*, and that there was a way out.

"When I visited my father for the last time, just before he died in hospital, I was able to focus more on how I could best help him and my mother come to terms with his impending death. We managed to talk very openly and intimately about our love for each other and say our farewells.

"And then, after his death, I took part in a special transference of consciousness, *puja* (special prayers) for my father with a group of local Buddhists, and also engaged in *Tara* (the female Bodhisattva of compassion) prayers for a few weeks after his death. I found that this helped enormously with the grieving process."

Still gently holding her husband's hand, Julie was leaning against the car that had brought them to the temple.

"How exactly did the puja help you?"

"It helped me not to focus on self-pity, but to focus more on my mother's feelings and my brother's and sister's feelings. After the transference of consciousness

I felt completely confident that my father had undertaken a fortunate rebirth. The night after the transference of consciousness, puja, I had extremely vivid dreams of what I took to be pure lands, places of such extraordinary beauty that I'd never actually seen in my waking life. There was a Buddha in it, and all sorts of things! That seemed to reinforce my conviction that my father had definitely benefited from the puja. I felt very happy."

As Julie seemed about to tell me even more about her progress, Dennis finally spoke. Extending his hand he said, "Thank you for listening. We didn't even ask but we assume you are also a Buddhist?" "Yes, I am, and it's been a great inspiration for me listening to your wife's experiences."

Silent for a moment as her husband ushered her into the car, Julie gave one of her radiant smiles, while taking time to look around at the throng of people leaving the temple grounds. "Great, isn't it?" she said. "Dhamma really works!"

Yes, I thought as their car crunched over the dusty gravel surface of the car park, it certainly does.

Righteous roots

Practising morality returns us
to the purity of our original nature

However carefully we follow
the teachings of the Buddha and try to make them part
of our daily lives through the practice and in the spirit of
Dhamma, we inevitably face times of doubt and self-
questioning. But by reminding ourselves of the basic
moral precepts, we can get back on track.

Let's think about these basic Buddhist moral precepts,
that guide our learning process and shape our development in Buddhist practice. The *Pali* term *sila*, which
more or less means morality, has its own set of ideas. It
denotes a state of normality, a condition which is basically
unqualified and pure. When we practise sila we return to

our basic state of untainted purity, our basic human nature where negative influences such as anger, greed, ill will and jealousy have no place. And as we practise, we are preserving the purity of our human nature.

We must also remind ourselves that on a personal level, the observance of precepts serves as the preliminary groundwork for the cultivation of higher virtues or mental development. Sila is indeed one of the most important steps on the spiritual path. Without morality, right concentration cannot be attained, and without right concentration, wisdom cannot be fully perfected. Morality not only enhances our ethical values; it is crucial to those of us who seek the highest goal of spiritual fulfilment.

Morality is always concerned with the issues of right and wrong, good and evil. For a moral life to be meaningful, these issues must not be only theoretical principles; they must be put into practice. Good must be done, evil must be given up. It is not enough to know what is good or evil, we also need to take proper action with respect to them. We need concrete guidelines to follow, and these are provided by the Buddhist moral precepts. Even the much-quoted Buddhist ideals of abstention from evil, doing what is good, can be made real simply by doing, by putting those principles into daily practice.

Buddhist moral precepts provide a wholesome foundation for personal and social growth. They are practical principles for a good life and the cultivation of good behaviour. If we understand the objectives of sila and realise its benefits, we will see moral precepts as an integral part of life, rather than as a burden to be shouldered. As individuals, we need to train in morality to lead a good and noble life. On the social level, we need to help maintain peace and harmony in society and work for the progress of the common good.

As we progress along the path of self-development we inevitably face moral dilemmas. How do we determine what is good and what isn't? The opposite of good may not necessarily be evil; but it is usually easy to distinguish right from wrong. To determine whether an action is good or evil, right or wrong, Buddhist ethics take into account three factors involved in a karmic that is, an intentional act. First, the intention itself that motivates the act; second, the act's effect on the doer; and third, the effect of the act on others. If the intention is good, motivated by love and compassion, if the result to the doer is wholesome (for instance, if it helps the doer to become more compassionate and unselfish), and if those to whom the act is directed also experience a positive result, then that act can be considered as good (*kusala*).

But if the act is rooted in negative mental qualities such as hatred and selfishness, if the result on the doer is negative and unpleasant, and if the receivers of the act also experience undesirable results or become more hateful and selfish, then that act is negative and without any benefit (*akusala*).

A particular act may appear to be a mixture of good and bad, in spite of the intention and the way it is performed. For instance, an act committed with the best of intentions may not bring the desired result for either the doer or the receiver. Sometimes an act based on negative intentions may produce apparently positive results (stealing, for instance, can bring wealth). We may confuse one set of actions with an unrelated set of results and make wrong conclusions, or simply misjudge them on account of preconceived social values and traditions. This can lead to wrong ideas about the law of karma, and loss of moral consciousness.

Buddhist moral precepts are based on the Dhamma, and they reflect such eternal values as compassion, respect, self-restraint, honesty and wisdom. These are values that are cherished and pursued by all civilisations, and their significance is universally recognised. Moral precepts that are based upon such values will always be relevant to human society. So, what are these Buddhist guiding precepts?

The first precept directs or advises us not to destroy life. This is based on the principle of goodwill and respect for the right to life of all living creatures including ourselves.

The second precept, not to take things which are not given, indicates respect for others' rights to possessions.

The third precept, not to indulge in sexual misconduct, warns against rape, adultery, and sexual promiscuity.

The fourth precept, not to tell lies or resort to false-hood, is an important factor in social life and dealings. It concerns respect for truth. The Buddha has said: "There are no evil deeds that a liar cannot do."

The last of the five Buddhist moral precepts directs us to avoid all intoxicants. On the personal level, absten-tion from intoxicants helps us to maintain mindfulness and a sense of responsibility. Socially, it helps to prevent accidents, on the road for instance, that can easily take place under the influence of alcohol or drugs.

The big picture

We must first know ourselves
in order to see
the world more clearly

Seeing the big picture, being able to view our world from a "fourth dimension" in our minds, is an amazingly effective way of developing what I would describe as practical Dhamma.

I was reminded of this as I returned to Bangkok by air from a recent upcountry trip. As the plane banked and prepared for its slow descent, I peered through the window for a glimpse of the world below. At first all I could see was part of the wing and a lot of sky. Then, as the aircraft turned again, quite suddenly there it was—the green and yellow chequered bedspread of the countryside.

As we descended, the geometric shapes dissolved to show ribbons of roads, the serpentine steel blue of the river, and soon, the slow-moving train of vehicles.

From this viewpoint I could see the whole panorama as it unfolded, and for that moment, as the aircraft held its course, the scene below conveyed all the purity and innocence of a child's picture book. I turned away, knowing that image would soon be shattered by the rush of warm air and the jet engine noise of the airport as the doors opened and another planeload of passengers was deposited back on terra firma.

But that fourth-dimension view, seeing the big picture, stayed with me as I looked out from the taxi at a now rain-soaked Bangkok. Later, as I caught up with the news, it helped me in my understanding as I read of more accounts of man's inhumanity to man.

Pondering all this, and looking at the often graphic television images of the injured, and bereaved, I was comforted by the realisation that horrific as these events were, they created a mere ripple on a much greater sea of tranquility and calm. And that sea, that continuum of time and space, of truth, of beauty and love, is in every one of us. Without beginning, without end. It simply is.

THE BIG PICTURE

But to know the big picture, the broad canvas painted with bold strokes and strong, contrasting colours, we must be able to understand the small picture, the detail. We cannot hope to achieve that elevated fourth dimension unless we first know ourselves.

That's why so much of the Buddha's teachings urge us to take a close look at ourselves. We may think we know so much about the world, about everything, and "how it all works", but how much do we know about ourselves, how we work? To help answer that question, Buddhism has given us two basic methods, both based on meditation—Vipassana and *Shamata* (concentration producing mental clam and clarity of the mind). These are commonly described, respectively, as "insight" and "calm abiding" meditation. Although initially they are often taught in sequence, with the idea being that first we must learn to calm our minds before we can benefit from a new level of understanding, the clarity of inner vision we will achieve, the two meditation methods are intended to work together, like one hand washing the other.

If we wish to see what is in a glass of swirling, muddy water, we set the glass down and let the dirt settle. Then we can see at a superficial level what is, and what is not, in the water. Taking that analogy further, the contents of the glass need to be analysed scientifically before all the various constituents can be identified. And that process can go on down to the subatomic level, and theoretically beyond.

The pursuit of knowledge and the ultimate understanding of how things are, can be a joyful process, and ultimately a joyous experience. When James Watson and Francis Crick discovered the structure of DNA, the basic molecule of life, in 1953, they were of course revealing a truth that had always existed. What they unravelled was a fantastically elegant process of genetic replication that was surely both immensely exciting and deeply moving as they pondered its implications.

They were asked, "How do the gene strands replicate themselves?" They answered, "Each strand has a molecular sound. This sound attracts the needed element and repels others."

Scientific confirmation indeed for the notion that each life-form has its own molecular sound. A unique symphony of life. A baby's laugh creates smiles for the listening parents. Sound has consequence.

As we look inside ourselves to discover our own truth with the help of Vipassana, we are not as seeking to negate all conscious thought, as sometimes is mistakenly believed. That would be pointless. From nothing comes nothing. Instead we seek to listen to the sounds of the universe that are within each one of us. To tune in to the vibrations of the eternal cycle of life and death. To understand the impermanence of all things, except Truth itself.

It was of course through meditation that the Buddha himself found enlightenment. In the course of his self-imposed introspection he was confronted by the dilemma that suffering in itself brings no more enlightenment than pleasure does.

He was tormented by desires as he contemplated what to do with his life; whether he should return to the vain pleasures of his earlier years, which he now saw to be ultimately pointless, or continue to suffer and deny himself pleasures, even though he now came to the realisation that this also brought no meaning into his life. Suddenly enlightenment came to the Prince, and at that moment he became the Buddha. Realising both the self-destructiveness of those who deny their desires and the misery of those who follow their desires, the Buddha also realised that there is a Middle Path, which is to simply lose one's desires. That is, an enlightened person should simply exist without desire.

A freed mind

Insight meditation teaches us to
embrace and live each moment to the full

"I need a break; if I go on like this I'll have a nervous breakdown." It's something we've all heard, or perhaps said, at one time or another. And often our friends or family members will encourage us. "Yes, a break will do you good, you'll be all the better for it, you'll come back raring to go."

At first glance it seems like good advice. It's certainly true that new sights and sounds can be quite refreshing, a change of pace can be very beneficial. But before we make arrangements for a long weekend at our favourite getaway we need to understand what it is we are escaping from.

When we refer to escaping we generally mean gaining our freedom from physical or mental restrictions. Our feeling for the need to escape, even temporarily, is partly the result of life's pressures, but mainly it arises because we aren't free in the present moment.

We may well benefit superficially from what we tell ourselves is a well-earned break. Often, though, it's nothing more than a distraction from the daily routine, from the prison we have made in our minds. How often, even on a comparatively long holiday, are our minds truly free? We may be enjoying the moment, the fresh sea breezes or the trek through the leafy forest, but a part of our mind constantly takes us back to our routine environment. "Will I have time to complete that report when I get back?" "I should have done my tax return before I left." "And grandmother, she was quite poorly, I hope she's OK I hope they remember to give her her medicine."

What then do we really mean by being "free in the present moment"?

It is about being awake to each experience in the moment and so consciously embracing life as fully as possible in our everyday experience.

But what is our ordinary, everyday experience? It's not just our awareness of external circumstances, or even such ordinary activities as walking, eating, sleeping, breathing, and speaking; it also includes our thinking and feeling: our ideas, moods, desires, passions, hopes and fears. In its most accessible form, ordinary, everyday experience is just how we feel at any particular moment.

It is in this moment that we find reality and freedom, for acceptance of life is acceptance of the present, now and at all times.

To allow this moment of experience, and all that it contains, the freedom to be as it is, to say what it has to say, to come and go in its own time, this is to allow the moment, which is where we always are, to set us free. And one of the ways we can achieve this is to practise Insight Meditation.

"Oh yes, that's something I've been meaning to pursue for a long time, but I'm always too busy. I have my job, and there's my family, and at weekends there's the tennis club and . . ." If you're one of the many well-meaning people who reacts in such a way when the subject of Insight Meditation is raised, then you are also in fact admitting you have yet to attain the clarity of vision and contentment that come from being free in the present moment.

When we practise Insight Meditation we pay clear attention to whatever exists naturally in this present moment. The specific focus for our awareness can vary, from bodily sensations to sights and sounds to thoughts and feelings. Often we begin by paying attention to the sensations of breathing. We sit still, either cross-legged on the floor or perhaps upright in a chair, and allow our eyes to close gently.

Then we turn our attention to the breath and simply experience, in as continuous a way as possible, the physical sensations of breathing in and breathing out. This simple activity of paying attention to our experience in the present moment is what the Buddha called "mindfulness". Mindfulness is the heart of Insight Meditation.

But meditation is not restricted to the special surroundings of a meditation centre, or even the quiet atmosphere of a special room in our house. It can also be carried on throughout our daily activities. We can be mindful of the movement of our body, the sensations experienced in walking, the sounds around us, or the thoughts and feelings that come into our mind.

And as our meditation practice develops, we find that the mind becomes calmer and clearer. We start to see the influence of our habitual patterns of moods, expectations, hopes and fears. In seeing through the mind's conditioning, we can live more fully in the present moment with all the benefits of clarity, compassion and understanding it brings.

This is the first taste of freedom. We are fully in touch with our experience of life, but we are not limited by it. We find we can manage the ups and downs of daily life more easily. We become more tolerant even in situations where normally we might respond angrily. We begin to see the truth within us.

Does this mean then that by achieving the freedom offered by Insight Meditation we will no longer find the need to take a break from our usual routine? Whether we do or not is entirely up to us. But if we do, it will be simply because we think it's a good idea, not because we are escaping from our own confusion. Wherever we are and whatever we're doing, whether relaxing on that breezy seashore, trekking through the forest or handling a tricky problem at work, we experience it with a free spirit and open heart.

One of the most well known quotations of the Buddha says, "Do not dwell in the past, do not dream of the future, concentrate the mind on the present moment." If we do that, the moment will always be ours.

Blind faith

**True wisdom means to directly see
and understand for ourselves**

Have you ever wondered why our beliefs and dogmas, especially religious ones, seem to have more to do with geography, which part of the world we live in, than with our thinking things out for ourselves?

Would the millions who follow one faith in a country where that faith is dominant, still follow that faith if they had been born in a country where another religion holds sway? Did they come to their beliefs after careful questioning, after thinking for themselves, or did they simply follow tradition, accepting the teaching of others as the ultimate wisdom?

Not questioning what are often presented to us as facts is not restricted to matters of religious faith. Most of us can think of examples of "facts" that we heard as children that we accepted, and perhaps in our ignorance even now still believe. Ideas about health and medical matters, for instance.

Have you ever been advised, perhaps by well-meaning friends, to tilt your head back when you've had a nose-bleed? Well, that would have been bad advice—doctors have long advised against what may seem a common-sense procedure. Tilting your head back can cause the blood to drain into the throat, which may cause choking or vomiting.

Or you may have been told that sudden changes of temperature, for instance when shoppers trudge from one air-conditioned shop to the next, or getting a thorough *Songkran* soaking, will give you a bad cold or even the dreaded flu. Not so—colds and flu are caused by a virus; all the available research demonstrates that a sudden change in temperature, or even going outside without thoroughly drying your hair after a shower, have nothing at all to do with it.

Sometimes we believe in things simply because they seem quite plausible, the idea that we'll likely catch a cold after a soaking for instance, or that eating too much sugar will give us diabetes. Together with the half-truths and plain falsehoods, there's a mass of misinformation that persists and seems self-perpetuating. And many people the world over still cling to superstition. Wiser observers may recognise these ideas for what they are and perhaps have fun ridiculing them; others who regard themselves as rational seem happy to defy logic and still believe there's some truth in such ideas.

"If a black cat walks towards you, it brings good fortune, but if it walks away, it takes the good luck with it." This is a belief common to many cultures, in the same category as "You must get out of bed on the same side that you get in, or you'll have bad luck," or "If you blow out all the candles on your birthday cake with the first puff, you'll get your wish."

Superstition, old wives' tales, folklore and these days, urban legends, can only exist in our minds when we don't think for ourselves, when we accept what others tell us without questioning. The Buddha encouraged us to question and analyse his teachings because he understood from his own experience that truth and the wisdom that comes from it can only be attained by looking for it.

Today there is much debate between national leaders about the rights and wrongs of going to war against a nation whose leader is perceived as being a threat to international security.

On both sides of the argument there is propaganda, misinformation and more insidiously, disinformation. Although what we think may have little effect on the outcome, this is an example of an issue where we should weigh carefully what we believe to be the facts and come to our own conclusion.

It is not wisdom if we simply believe what we are told. True wisdom is seeing directly and understanding for ourselves. It also means being open to new ideas, accepting or rejecting them only after careful consideration, and then always being open to re-examining them. And we must especially be prepared to admit the error of our thinking when we are proved wrong.

Achieving that degree of wisdom is not easy. It requires courage, patience, flexibility and intelligence. It also brings with it great rewards. Without wisdom, for instance when we exercise compassion and show loving kindness to others, we are simply being kindhearted fools. The wisdom that comes from right thinking—seeing things as they really are and accepting the impermanence of all things—allows us to live without the craving that causes suffering and the self-delusion that comes from false ideas.

So how do we achieve this wisdom in our everyday lives? Indeed, it takes time, a great deal of study, and perhaps even a teacher. After all, how can we learn if we don't even know what questions to ask? How can we even begin when we have to work every day to support ourselves and our families?

The Buddha would say that the wisdom we seek is within ourselves. If we begin by ridding our minds of selfish desires, this is the first step, not only to escape from suffering, but to allow that wisdom to reveal itself. And when it does, we'll recognise its truth and purity.

Theory into practice

**The means to free ourselves
is always there if we look hard enough**

Have you ever noticed that when someone tells you a story, especially if it's offered as a humorous contribution, it is often especially revealing about the storyteller? We have all been surprised, for instance, when a straight-laced colleague tells a joke seemingly completely out of character, or when the office clown shows a serious side of his character with a thought-provoking account of a personal incident about which we were all completely unaware.

Usually these "revelations" take place at some get-together when people are feeling relaxed. Such occasions are not only entertaining, they are often therapeutic, allowing us to get things off our chest the way an actor does in playing a part. They can also be educational, as was a recent weekend "away from it all" that I recently shared with a group of colleagues. It wasn't a retreat in the meditative sense, although the woodland setting and the rustic accommodation offered an ideal atmosphere for introspection. It was simply meant to be a chance to escape the decibel din and polluted air, and to enjoy the real or perceived benefits of sleeping under mosquito nets; of washing in the cool (actually freezing) water of the nearby stream, and hiking up mountain trails, worn to a slippery smoothness by the rugged footwear of a thousand tourists.

And at the end of the day, that time of aching limbs and weary minds, came the story-telling. There was no escape. Those who attempted to sneak off would be called back to the fold with cries of "Come on, come on. Everybody has to join in."

The unofficial leader of our get-together had wisely ruled that our story-telling session should follow certain loose guidelines. It was therefore decreed and agreed upon that contributions should have more than simply entertainment value. They should, in the long established tradition of such tales, have a moral.

I thought it would be fun and even instructive if I recounted a couple of the stories as I remember them.

The first concerns a young, highly educated professor of physics who decided he would take time off in the tradition of the seventh-year sabbatical. He would take a sea voyage around the world, exchanging the classroom for the ship's deck. The ocean would be his mentor, the starlit sky his inspiration.

But he couldn't give up his natural inclination to pass on his wisdom, and every evening he gave a short talk on one subject or another to an audience of passengers and crew. After one talk in which he discussed the importance of oceanography, he was approached by an old sailor. "What's all this about what you call oceanography, Professor? It's all I can do to pronounce it, let alone understand it." "Well, my good man," said the professor, "it's just one of the many subjects you should master if you make your living as a sailor. What about astronomy, for instance, meteorology, and these days, navigation technology?" "Don't know nothing about those things either, Professor. I never learnt to read or write properly. What I know, I know." "But you have to understand the science and the theory behind what you do." "Oh, I leave all that to others. All those 'onomies and 'ologies, I'll never get my head round those. Anyway, thanks for your time Professor, I've got some work to do before I turn in."

Later that very night the professor was awakened by a thunderous noise and seconds after, a frantic knocking on his cabin door. There was the old sailor, holding a life-jacket. "Professor, what do you know about swim-mology?" "What? What's going on? What do you mean, swimmology?" "Can you swim, Professor?" "Well, of course, I have a comprehensive knowledge of the theory, it's all a matter of . . ." "But can you swim? The ship's run aground. We've hit a rock, and we're sinking." The old sailor thrust the lifejacket at the bewildered academic. "Put this on and follow me. I'll help you into a lifeboat— what you might call survivology."

And the moral of that little tale of the sea is that how-ever much we understand the teachings of the Buddha, of Loving Kindness and Compassion for instance, that knowledge will have no effect on our lives, or the lives of others, unless we put theory into practice.

Here's another tale with a twist contributed by the oldest member of our group. In an area where the law was in the hands of a ruling clique who would routinely imprison their opponents on false charges, yet another protester was hauled off in the middle of the night and thrown into the dungeons of the old castle that served as the jail.

"You've got to get me out of here," he said to the only visitor he was allowed, a monk from the local temple. "Be patient, I will bring you something that will help you," said the monk. He had to wait another month for the monk's next visit but this time his visitor left him a parcel with the words, "Make full use of this and you will gain your freedom." Obviously it had been scrutinised by the guards so he had little hope of it containing anything of much use. And when he saw that it was just a prayer mat, his disappointment quickly turned to anger. What good is this, he asked himself, unless it contains something of practical value, something to blast a hole in the wall for instance, or some high-tech device that would cut through the steel door of his cell. But it was just what it appeared to be—a simple prayer mat.

One day he picked it up and noticed it appeared to have some kind of pattern on it. He studied it carefully, holding it up to the only source of light, a narrow slit in the old castle wall. He could only make out a few faint lines but they did seem to be part of some kind of diagram.

Over the next many days, spurred by the possibility that the mat contained some kind of secret message, and remembering the monk's words that if he used the mat, he would gain his freedom, he studied it from every angle, but try as he could, he saw only the same faint outline. "Perhaps I should really use it, after all that's what the monk actually said." So that night, in the semi-darkness, he unrolled the mat, and closing his eyes, began to pray for understanding. He remained in silent prayer for a long while and finally opened his eyes. As he did so, he saw that the lines on the mat, that had been until then barely discernible, were absolutely clear. They had been drawn in luminous paint. He was looking at a detailed diagram of an escape route accessible from a secret opening in his dungeon wall.

I hardly need point out that the moral here is that for each of us, however much we feel imprisoned by life's misfortunes and the suffering we must endure, the means to free ourselves is always there if we look hard enough.

Elusive search

Taking the middle path
can help us avoid conflict and
move closer to ultimate truth

Since the very earliest times
humanity has wrestled with the concept of truth. It has
occupied the finest minds and formed the basis of a whole
body of philosophical thinking.

The need for each one of us to be steadfast in our
commitment to leading our lives based on the fundamental truths of existence is increasingly important today
when the values that come from that commitment are
being challenged at every level.

How then do we define truth, both in its broadest terms and how it applies to living and working in the day-to-day world in which we are all involved?

At the practical level, we might say truth is the reality of nature, the cycle of birth and death of all living things. The truth of night and day, of heat and cold, of desire and suffering, of sadness and discontent, and the uplifting joy and understanding that comes from the ultimate truth of love and compassion.

In its broadest sense, we might also say truth is that which is. However and wherever we look for truth, it remains unchanged. It is the eternal constant. Paradoxically, when we search for the truth, we are not always ready to receive it. If we open our minds in love and a desire to see things as they are, truth will find us.

Opening our minds, however, means more than sitting passively in our favourite chair, closing our eyes and saying something like, "Let the truth come in." Rather than having any great revelation, we are more likely to nod off to sleep. First, we need to understand the distinction between what some Buddhist scholars have called Relative Truth and Ultimate Truth. Relative truths describe what we generally regard as facts: the sun rises in the east, sets in the west, there are seven days in a week, the shortest distance between two points is a straight line, and if we go for a long time without eating, we feel hungry.

Surely, we might say, those facts and many others that we have come to accept as being indisputable are more than relative? After all, the sun does rise in the east and does set in the west; we all know that, we can see it with our own eyes. The answer, of course, is that such truths are relative because the way we perceive them relates to our own experience. The sun only appears to rise and set as it does because of its position relative to the earth; days, weeks, months, years are only terms we have evolved to provide a way of communicating ideas about the passage of time. Relative truths such as these and the millions of others that exist, form a vast interdependent network, a basic framework of information and knowledge that serves as an essential source of reference for us to manage our lives.

Although we clearly need this bank of information, of relative truths, to be able to function in today's world, we must also remind ourselves that those truths exist only in relation to one another, that they have no real identity, no actual existence in themselves.

What then of Ultimate Truth, does that exist? Simply by searching for it we acknowledge that it exists, our search itself is part of the Ultimate Truth. Does this mean that to lead a happy and fulfilling life we should devote ourselves to discovering the Truth? If we wish to pursue such a course, we are free to do so and we need look no further than within ourselves.

Nevertheless, whether we spend every thinking moment exploring the profound questions of our existence and the nature of reality or think only of such imponderables in moments of quiet contemplation, or in the few minutes before our favourite TV programme, the truth is always there for us to see. And when we do see the truth we will realise that by constantly searching for a meaning in life we are actually creating the opposite, a state of confusion leading to suffering and unhappiness.

We are often reminded that the Dhamma of the Buddha is one of a middle way, and we may think of this as meaning that we should avoid extremes of behaviour, of clinging too much to one pleasure or another—that we should take the middle path. This is certainly a valid interpretation, but by advocating the middle way the Buddha also meant that we should reject the extremes in the way we think about the meaning of our existence and the way this too, can affect our daily lives. We tend to think, for example, of people being good or bad and may say that people are basically good, or we may express the opposite and say that people are basically evil. Neither of these views represents reality, they are simply ideas, concepts. Clearly, taking the middle path is more logical; it is also closer to reality.

For us to begin fearlessly to take the middle path we must truly accept the reality of truth as the arising and ceasing of existence as it is as this moment. When we grasp that reality, we will see that the confusion that arises in our search for that elusive truth becomes irrelevant, and once free from that confusion we become a step closer to achieving the ultimate freedom that comes from seeing things as they really are.

So what does this all mean to us in this world today? How will an understanding of reality help us to cope when even now conflicts continue to threaten the lives of people and the very existence of independent nations? A clear understanding of the Buddhist concepts of Relative and Ultimate Truths will allow each one of us to realise that those very conflicts arise from reasoning based on Relative Truths, and thus have no foundation in reality. That understanding can guide us in all our relationships with others as we progress along the middle path.

DHAMMA TEACHINGS

Dhamma in the workplace

Shallow society

An obsession with looks
distracts from the true meaning of life

One of the most beautiful faces I have seen recently belonged to a young lady in my office who had returned from a 10-day Vipassana meditation retreat. She had been troubled by many personal problems, both imagined and to her at least, very real.

Like many young women of her age she tried to make herself look as attractive as possible. A bit on the plump side, she was an avid follower of all the latest slimming fads, trying out facial creams and other beauty preparations. Sadly none of them seemed to work for her. In fact the application of one particular lotion caused a reaction which required medical attention.

Naturally she became depressed, which in turn made her irritable and bad tempered. So, she became unattractive externally, both physically and in her personality. Internally, she was tormented by emotions of dissatisfaction, frustration, and finally self-loathing. And perversely, she turned to food for comfort—cakes and pastries, sweets and biscuits soon became her daily diet.

My first reaction was a desire to help, but especially as a man, I knew I would have to tread carefully. I also knew that basically she would describe herself as a Buddhist, while probably admitting she gave only lip service to the teachings of the Buddha.

One day I resolved to put my compassion into practice. "There's a great new vegetarian restaurant open just at the end of our soi. Come on, let's try it out for lunch." Although she protested, she finally gave in, and soon I had her more or less to myself in the restaurant which was not yet very busy.

I began with what I hoped was a tactful way of getting to the point of my little ruse. "Tell me, how would you define beauty?" "Look, I know you're trying to cheer me up," she said, trying her best to look grateful, and giving me a half-hearted smile. "You're going to tell me that beauty is actually more than skin deep, and I should start thinking all kinds of beautiful thoughts, have a good night's sleep and I'll wake up looking like a fresh-faced teenager."

It was my turn to smile, in fact I chuckled loudly. "Well not exactly, although I would certainly say that external beauty can only come from within. We really are what we think. And clearly how we perceive ourselves makes all the difference as to how we appear to others." "So you're saying to look beautiful, I have to think of myself as being beautiful," she said. "Yes, but there's more to it than that. We've already mentioned that old saying about beauty being only skin deep. Let's look at another saying, the one about beauty being in the eye of the beholder. Don't you think we can apply this to many different types of beauty, apart from the obvious physical kind?"

We were halfway through our lunch, but I was now beginning to gain her full attention. We talked about the beauty of the arts, of painting, of music, of literature and of knowledge itself. "Real beauty," I said, "comes from within. It is the beauty of Dhamma in body, speech, and mind."

We talked some more on this theme, and soon my young colleague was coming up with examples of her own. "You know, there's an old noodle seller in the *soi* where I live. I see her almost every day and she always seems to have a smile on her face, even when she has no customers. She must be over 80, but her face has a sort of radiance. I often wonder what she's got to be happy about. She looks like she's just won the lottery." "And I bet she doesn't wear makeup," I chipped in.

It would soon be time to get back to the office, but I knew most of my Dhamma work was done. In the restaurant's foyer there was a large mirror and as we left I took my colleague's arm and steered her towards the mirror. "Do me a favour, take a look at yourself and tell me what you see." Smiling slightly, she did as I asked. Even as she studied her reflection, she couldn't prevent the smile developing into a wide grin, and finally a happy laugh.

As we walked back to the office she suddenly tugged my arm, "You know what, you got me thinking and talking so much I forgot to eat my dessert, and it was my favourite carrot cake and creamy sauce."

From the very next day we all noticed a marked change in our young colleague's appearance. Although she still bore signs of the allergic reaction on her face, she appeared much less concerned. She seemed to radiate a sort of quiet optimism and was almost determinedly cheerful.

A week later she came to see me. "It's my turn to treat you to lunch, what do you fancy?" We settled for noodles, and soon we were trying to catch each other's words over the lunchtime clatter and conversation buzz of the noodle shop. "I have something to tell you. Actually you're the first to know—I haven't even told my parents yet."

Perhaps she's about to get married, or leave to work abroad, I thought. "Well, after our discussion last week about beauty, I realised that I'd got it all wrong. You know, I read about the extreme lengths some people go to achieve what they perceive as beauty and I felt I wanted to rush out and tell them how misguided they were."

"Is that what you wanted to tell me?" "No, that's just how I feel. You know, I have a couple of weeks' holiday coming up, well, I've decided to use it to go on a meditation retreat. I'm putting your advice into practice."

I was of course flattered, but most of all thrilled. My gentle prodding had helped bring her back to the path of self-realisation; the rest, as they say, would be up to her.

SHALLOW SOCIETY

A few weeks later I heard a slight cough and when I looked up, there she was. Yes, she was slimmer, but the most obvious change was in her face. She appeared at once serene yet radiant. Quite simply, beautiful. Her inner happiness was clearly evident as she smiled and handed me a single apple. "For your dessert," she said.

Millionaires seldom smile

Giving to others should always be done
without expecting anything in return

Who wants to be a million-
aire? The title of that old song often comes to my mind
as I observe the people that make up what most of us
refer to as high society. It's probably fair to say that you
don't have to be a millionaire or even very rich to be a
high-so celebrity. It's probably also true to say that having
money certainly helps.

You know how it is. You remember the first few lines
of a song and because they touch a chord somewhere in
your psyche you often sing them to yourself like a mantra,
especially if the tune is also catchy. "Who wants to be a

millionaire, wallow in champagne, have a fancy yacht and a supersonic plane" . . . I was singing to myself very quietly at a particular glittering gathering when a colleague came along and neatly added his own version of the next line, "I do, I do," he sang, and moved away smiling, before I could say anything.

A while later I spotted him again. He was still smiling and when he saw me he beckoned me over. He nodded to a particularly attractive and elegant young woman across the room. "Money can't buy me love," he began. We both enjoyed the joke. It's also been said that it can't buy happiness or health, and I was thinking of this old adage and the many others associated with this most basic of human needs when I got home.

How does the idea of making money equate with my Buddhist beliefs, I asked myself. After all, we need money to survive, and what can be wrong in creating wealth, a strong, prosperous society, with equal opportunities for everybody? With these ideas running through my mind, I decided to look up a few facts about millionaires. Just for fun, the first thing I did was to turn to an old song book from my student days for the actual lyrics of that song that had started me off earlier in the evening.

To my surprise, far from singing the praises of the life of a millionaire, the light-hearted lyrics by Cole Porter actually do the opposite. "Who wants a fancy foreign car? I don't. Who wants to tire of caviar? I don't," are typical of the lines of the song.

And as for miserable and reputedly miserly millionaires, there seem to have been plenty of them around in the past, and these days it also seems that the more millionaires there are, the less merry they become.

It's not surprising when we think about it. As people make more and more money, they are able to surround themselves with the material wealth they have long yearned for. A luxurious house, servants, not one but several cars, all the latest gadgets—it's a familiar scenario.

Often they are proud of their material success and show off their expensive lifestyle. And often too they become attached to their possessions, so much so they are in constant fear that they may lose them. They become prisoners of their avarice.

There are also the miserly millionaires who in spite of their vast wealth never tip, pay their staff the least they can get away with, and spend little, even on themselves. Of such a kind were a family I read about, who although they had received a huge inheritance from their parents, spent very little of it. The six sisters and one brother lived in the same house for 50 years. None of them married, and when the last sister died, the estate was valued at hundreds of millions of dollars. Her only dress was one that she had made herself, and she had worn it for 25 years.

It's clear enough that a life spent entirely in the pursuit of wealth in the form of material possessions can leave very little time for much else. So, we need to see money for what it really is—a means to an end, not the end itself. The end we seek to achieve will vary according to our circumstances, but it should always be to live a happy and contented life, showing generosity and kindness to others—and we don't need to be a millionaire to do that.

Here's a quote I came across which I believe sums up neatly what money can and cannot do for us: "Money will buy a bed, but not sleep; books, but not brains; food, but not appetite; finery, but not beauty; a house, but not a home; medicine, but not health; luxuries, but not culture; amusements, but not happiness."

Not so long ago a prominent Buddhist temple was in the news for what some described as commercialisation of the traditional practice of merit-making. Followers, it was said, were being encouraged by the use of modern advertising techniques to donate as much money as possible to the temple to pay for elaborate buildings. A well known academic commented at the time, "Ask yourself what's the real purpose in going to the temple, to be peaceful in mind, or to see a sort of splendid construction, or colourful architecture? Why pay so much? Remember 'merit' does not mean giving your money."

Giving to others should always be done without expecting anything in return. We can give in many ways, including offering our services, providing material gifts or donating money itself. Giving also requires that it be done with a pure heart and this means being glad to give before giving, believing in giving while actually giving, and taking delight afterwards in having given. Merit comes not from the giving or the gift but from the intention of the giver.

And those millionaires? Here's what two old-timers had to say: "I was happier when doing a mechanic's job," said Henry Ford. And from Andrew Carnegie, "Millionaires seldom smile." In a nutshell, money can't buy many things, including happiness.

Dhamma at work

The need to cultivate relationships is based on mutual respect

Most of us spend a great proportion of our adult life in some form of employment, and whether we run our own business, work for a small or large company or even work from an office at home, we need to be able to get on with other people. They may be our office colleagues, the company managing director, the cleaning lady or our customers; they are all people we have to relate to in a work environment, and how we handle our relationships with each of them can make all the difference between happiness and discontent.

The typical office environment is one in which many of us have firsthand experience, and it often seems to take up a disproportionate part of our life. We get in early to avoid the traffic, to impress the boss, to set a good example or simply to get our work done, and increasingly we leave late, often for the same reasons. And as we become more and more resentful at how work and all its problems seems to be taking over our lives, we begin to ask ourselves, "Is it all worth it? Why am I doing this?" Often the answer is that we appear to have no choice. We need the money, we say, and resign ourselves to what has become a daily drudge.

Clearly there's something wrong. Life shouldn't be like that, and it doesn't have to be. Many, if not most of the work-related problems we face in the office and other similar environments are about relationships; specifically, relationships which are not working properly and which cause disharmony, distress and all-round dissatisfaction. In other words, people problems. How we get on with one another?

People who make a living from giving advice on how other people should best be managed in the work environment, used to ask questions about whether a particular individual was a good team player, able to work on their own initiative, respect the views of others. Now they talk about EQ, Emotional Quotient. For years most of us have been familiar with IQ, our Intelligence Quotient—our ability to understand factual knowledge, our verbal and mathematical skills, our memory and powers of logical reasoning.

The now fashionable EQ refers to our ability to deal with emotions and feelings in others as well as ourselves, which is the secret of all human relationships. The present thinking is that EQ can predict success in life and work better than IQ can. In conventional psychological terms this may well be so, but however accurately it describes our emotional skills, isn't it just another way of describing what I prefer to call "Dhamma at Work" and the benefits of its practical application?

Here in Thailand the many work-related problems are made more complicated by, or stem directly from, the inevitable differences in cultural attitudes between western and Thai people. Situations that are tolerated or which are manageable in a social context can lead to a crisis in a business environment. This problem of differ-ent cultural attitudes goes much deeper than understanding what might be described as the subtleties of social etiquette in the office context, a subject regularly covered in the business columns of newspapers where the conventional wisdom of mutual understanding and tolerance is the order of the day. We have to do more than simply attempt to develop mutual understanding. We need to cultivate relationships based on mutual respect.

Let's first look at some of the common sources of office conflict and disharmony. Broadly speaking, they can be thought of as colleague problems and boss problems.

Conflicts, disagreements and plain old mutual dislike among colleagues are, some might say, to be expected and even accepted as the price of having a job. The same problems with a boss—someone who has the power to hire and fire—can be that much more difficult to deal with. There's the bossy boss, the aloof and unfriendly boss, and the too-friendly boss, the slave-driving boss and the boss who's never there when needed. Then perhaps worst of all, there's the boss who is always the first to arrive, the last to leave, and who makes it clear that everybody else is expected to do the same. The implication is that those who don't will be considered disloyal.

There's not enough space here to explore specific problems and how to deal with them, but let's look at one real-life example that I witnessed in the early days of my own career.

The managing director of the company was of the first-to-arrive, last-to-leave type. He was also set in his ways, wary of new ideas, believed he knew best, and even in discussion with senior employees would treat their views with derision and sarcasm. Those who were bold enough to leave at the normal time would be subjected to an icy stare or comments such as, "Before you go to your party, please make sure you complete the report you're working on."

And it was one of those senior employees, Mr David, who had earlier been very supportive of the managing director and provided valuable assistance in dealing with the company's clients, who finally decided enough was enough. He began to come into the office late in the day, eventually saying he preferred to work from home. When this didn't work out, he left.

A few weeks after he had left the company I caught up with him at a business event and he seemed eager to share his feelings of being treated badly by someone with whom he had once enjoyed a friendly working relationship. He seemed hurt and even angry, saying that he hoped others would not share his fate.

Back in the office the routine of work went on much as usual, but I did notice that the boss was more subdued. He seemed determined to work even harder, but appeared to have decided to be less critical of others. It wasn't a happy atmosphere, but there was less tension, and when it was time to go home at the end of the day people would leave without drawing managerial comment.

Then one day, quite unexpectedly, Mr David walked in and knocked on the managing director's office. We heard the "May I come in?" and the door closed. They talked for an hour or more. Later we heard that Mr David had decided it was not sensible or right for either of them to harbour such mutual ill feelings, and that they had agreed they had both been at fault and resolved to re-establish their friendly relationship. He never did come back to work in the office, but the results of his initiative were clear to see in the much better attitude of the managing director.

Dealing with the dragons at work

A friendly, team approach
will often work wonders

There's something about saying "Good morning," especially to colleagues at work, that seems to present a real problem for some people. This is particularly true, it seems, for bosses and supervisors. It's all part of what I call the po-faced syndrome, and it seems to afflict managers and supervisors particularly severely.

You know the scenario. A group of workers pause to exchange a few pleasantries or to share a joke, when their immediate boss walks by with a disapproving glare or perhaps stops to deliver an ultimatum about a certain task having to be completed on time. "You can sit around gossiping all day, but that report has to be on my desk by nine o'clock tomorrow morning, even if you have to work all night."

The negative effects of this attitude are obvious, and it's a mystery why those who behave that way can't see how counterproductive it really is. The first thing that happens is that those who have been chastised feel resentful. They return to their work muttering among themselves and harbouring unpleasant thoughts about their boss, perhaps even agreeing not to finish the job on time, just to "pay him back".

How different could it have been had the boss greeted them with a smile and said something like "Good morning, everyone. You all seem to be in a cheerful mood. By the way, please don't forget we have a nine o'clock deadline for this job tomorrow morning. Let me know if you run up against any problems. Anyway, you've made a good start. See you all later."

Apart from being friendly, positive and encouraging, using a phrase such as "We have a nine o'clock deadline" makes it clear that everyone including the boss is part of the same team with a common objective. It also confirms that help will be available if any problems arise. Clearly, this is the right kind of motivation. To be really effective, however, it must also be sincere and not just smooth talk turned on when necessary. That old adage about being able to fool some people some of the time is simply not true. No one is fooled by insincerity, except perhaps those who indulge in it.

Fortunately, the po-faced syndrome is not always what it seems. How often have we looked on a person as surly, unfriendly and even hostile, only to discover that they are in fact none of these, but simply shy?

There was Arthur, for example, the security guard at a company I worked for during the early part of my career. Always serious-looking with the air of a parade ground sergeant-major, he would make everyone feel uncomfortable simply by appearing on his rounds or being at his post when we left the building. We all accepted that he had an important job to do, but we wished that just once in a while he would behave less like a robot and more like a human being.

Then one weekend I bumped into him, almost literally, in the supermarket. That was the first time I had seen him out of uniform, and it was quite a surprise. He had two lively young children with him, and he appeared to be doing the family shopping. I couldn't avoid saying something, as he'd obviously seen me.

"Hello, Arthur, lovely children. Are they yours?" From its usual mask of impassive politeness, his face changed instantly into that of a proud father, the friendly neighbour, and a man you would want to be your friend. With a broad smile he said, "Indeed, they're a bit of a handful, but I bring them here every Saturday while my wife goes to her coffee morning."

We chatted pleasantly for a while about nothing in particular before getting on with our own Saturday shopping chores. As I left the store I could see Arthur studying the shelves in his typical methodical way while keeping a fatherly eye on his children. This time, though, there was a difference. He was still displaying that proud, happy smile.

The following Monday morning, encouraged by our Saturday encounter, I felt bold enough to venture a "Good morning, Arthur, how are you today?" There was that smile again, and the friendly reply, "Very well, Sir, and thank you for asking." Arthur's secret was out. He was simply an old softie who gave the impression of being a real terror because he felt that was what his job demanded.

The point here is that many of the dragons we encounter at work aren't really dragons at all, and those that are unpleasant, bossy and intimidating can be tamed with understanding and compassion. Whatever drives their behaviour, whether it's a genuine desire to get the work done or part of their personal career strategy, its cause is their own lack of confidence. They believe that being anything other than a tough slave-driver is the only way. Showing any form of friendliness to those under their authority would, in their eyes, be a sure sign of weakness.

Changing their attitude is not easy, but its always worth the effort. And what's the secret to this magical metamorphosis? Charm, cheerfulness, and a large helping of compassion. Charm, because even surly, unfriendly and domineering bosses do respond to sincere flattery. "Do you have a few minutes? We would really appreciate your advice on how to approach this job. We know you've had a lot of experience in this area."

Cheerfulness, because if the dragon approach is met with a cheerful remark such as "Actually, with your help we plan to have the whole job finished by this afternoon", the fire will soon fizzle out.

And compassion, because those with the po-faced syndrome generally have many problems of their own, perhaps such as insecurity and low self-esteem.

Remember, a cheery "Good morning", works wonders both for those on the receiving end and the person who volunteers it. By the way, there's also nothing to stop you from offering an equally cheery "See you tomorrow," at the end of the working day.

I'm sure Arthur would approve.

Maximum benefits

The Lord Buddha offered
sound economic advice in his teachings

Every day we're bombarded
with information about economics. Every newspaper has
pages devoted to it, every television or radio newscast
includes some sort of business section where the latest
economic developments around the world are discussed
and analysed.

Immersed in our daily lives, most of us take little
interest in talk of balance of payments, inflation, cost of
living indices and the like. We may well believe that
economics has little to do with us, and even that as
Buddhists we shouldn't be concerned with such things,

viewing the whole world of business as unwholesome, something to be avoided.

The reality of course is that we simply cannot avoid it. Whatever we do, however simply we live, each of us is an integral part of the system. If we can't escape the all-embracing consequences of what is now called the science of economics, can we adopt its principles to reflect our Buddhist beliefs? Can there in fact be such a thing as Buddhist Economics?

If we accept that economics is in fact a science, should it not play a major role in benefiting humanity, helping to create prosperous and harmonious societies, bringing stability and an acceptable standard of living to all? Obviously the answer is yes, it should, and equally obviously we can see that it fails to do so.

Conventional economics fails because its objectives are narrow and it takes no account of ethical values. To an economist a bottle of whisky and a book advocating the application of Buddhist principles in business have the same economic value. The potential damaging effects of alcohol to individuals and society in general or the benefits of Buddhist-based business policies, play little or no part in the decision to open a liquor store or a bookshop.

From a Buddhist perspective, economics cannot be viewed as a specialist area of knowledge. Rather it must be seen as one of a number of interdependent disciplines working in concert towards the common goal of social, individual and environmental well-being.

Long before economics evolved as a science, the Buddha set out several principles for sound economic practice, and even in today's world of multi-national corporations and macro-economics, these principles still hold true and can be applied equally to big business or to our various individual situations.

The first of these principles says that when we work to acquire wealth we must do it in an ethical way, not taking advantage of others or engaging in work or business that is not Right Livelihood, that is in Dhamma language Unwholesome. Included in this list for example would be trading in arms and weaponry or in people, selling live animals to the slaughterhouse, trading in alcohol and other intoxicants, and making a living out of charging interest on loans.

In one of his birthday messages, His Majesty the King urged every one of us to do our bit in helping to combat the menace of drugs. His Majesty knows only too well that the success or failure of this evil business is in the hands of those who suffer most from it—the end users. No business can survive without customers.

Young people especially should be encouraged to follow the Eightfold Path and live their lives according to the Five Precepts. This simple act alone will ensure there are no more customers for the drug peddlers.

The second of the Buddha's economic principles concerned the importance of careful conservation of the money and wealth we acquire; of the wisdom of putting some aside for a rainy day—of spending our money wisely and not on an extravagant and self-indulgent lifestyle.

Living within one's means is the thrust of the third principle. Today, when so many young people get themselves into debt by overspending with their credit cards, this commonsense dictum is especially relevant.

The fourth piece of sound advice from the Buddha is to cultivate a network of the right kind of friends in our lives. The importance of this virtue was stressed by the Buddha, who especially in the context of economics, taught that simply acquiring, storing and using wealth isn't good enough. We have to build up a network of good people to work with too, before we get round to using our wealth. The Buddha also emphasised that in earning our living, we should try to avoid associating with those who break the Precepts.

The advice the Buddha gave on matters relating to economics was amazingly practical, even to the extent of recommending how the family budget should be divided and managed. One part, he said should be reserved for the needs of your family and household; one part to extend generosity to our friends; one part to be saved for a rainy day or an emergency; one part for charitable causes; and one part towards supporting monks.

But, you might say, some people hardly earn enough to survive; how can they possibly begin to even think about saving? Some are driven to stealing or other types of crime simply to feed their children. You feel sorry for them, you say, and blame the government, citing the low pay of officials for the rampant corruption we read about almost daily. Do you really believe that stealing, seeking and accepting bribes can be justified simply because an individual wants more, more than he or she can afford?

Fortunately there are still those stories that show the other side of the coin: Of diligent, hardworking parents doing menial jobs and living in the most simple circumstances, who struggle each day to feed, clothe and educate their children, instilling in them the virtues of honesty and truthfulness. Their economic management is based on sound principles, the principles of Buddhist Economics.

The best policy

The practice of honesty and integrity lies at
the heart of the principle of Right Speech

"Corporate America under
siege," "Big business in big trouble," "Dishonest account-
ing practices rife," say the headlines, and we all know
they are referring to the blight of scandals that have shaken
US business, with repercussions still reverberating around
the world.

And oddly, most observers seem not at all surprised.
"Business is like that," they say, almost as if attempting
to justify all the lying, stealing and rampant dishonesty.
It's easy enough to understand that attitude. It's all around
us. How many times have we heard the expression, "It's

nothing personal, it's just business," implying that disregard for the principles of honesty, integrity and fairness is acceptable, because, well, it's business.

Under this "It's only business" umbrella of acceptable practices, hypocrisy and humbug are the order of the day. While proclaiming an unswerving commitment to noble principles, businesses large and small continue to exploit their employees, paying them minimum wages, even in extreme cases using children and illegal immigrants as virtual slaves. They pay lip service to conserving the environment while releasing toxic waste into rivers and streams, they falsify invoices and receipts to cheat on their taxes, and in supreme irony, they can be seen making grand public gestures of charity.

Many of us, while despairing at what seems to be an ever growing conspiracy to seek to prosper at the expense of others, ask ourselves what we can do about it. After all, we might say, whatever we do as individuals will make no difference. We can't change the world.

In some ways business seems to be making serious attempts to put its own house in order, if not to change the world in which it operates. Long before the new century's scandals made headlines, the notion of Good

Corporate Governance and Corporate Social Responsibility were being promoted in boardrooms around the world. Sadly, this has not always been because it's the right thing to do, but because it's seen as being good for business.

In 1994 the Caux Round Table (the CRT) published its Principles for Business as a guide to business practices in an era of Globalisation. The CRT recommends use of these Principles in a *Theravada* society like Thailand as well as in societies living by other religious and cultural traditions.

The CRT Principles call for Thai and all other business leaders to implement certain rules of corporate governance, transparency, avoidance of corruption and crony favouritism, respect for the environment and fair treatment of customers and employees.

Of course there are many businesses that are run with integrity and honest intentions, guided perhaps by sincere personal beliefs and the CRT Principles, that don't seek to prosper at the expense of others and whose management is genuinely concerned at creating benefits for the community at large. Wherever they are, they are to be applauded and encouraged.

We may not be able to change the world, but what we can do as individuals is to encourage honesty and integrity by our own conduct. The practices of honesty and truthfulness are basic principles in all religions, and are at the very heart of Buddhism. They can be seen, for example, in the principle of Right Speech which urges abstinence from lies and deceptions, backbiting, idle talk and abusive speech. The cultivation of honesty and truthfulness; to practise speech that is kind and benevolent. To let our words reflect our desire to help, not harm others.

Right Action tells us to practise selfless conduct that reflects the highest statement of the life we want to live, and to conduct ourselves in a manner that is peaceful, honest and pure, showing compassion for all living beings.

Think for a moment what could happen if every individual in the world were to embrace those principles of honesty and truthfulness. Add compassion, a touch of tolerance, a dash of selflessness, a helping of loving kindness, and we have a recipe for true understanding. Could conflict and strife, between groups of individuals, between nations even, have any hope of surviving in such a world? I don't think so.

That is what we must strive for in everything we think, everything we say, everything we do.

THE BEST POLICY

Telling it as it is

**Euphemisms can obscure the truth
and should be treated with caution**

These days there seems to be a whole new vocabulary for many practices that have been going on for years. This seems especially so in the world of business, and many of us who work in this environment will be familiar enough with most of them. "Human resources", for example, which to me seems a decidedly less than human description, is now used to refer to people.

Companies speak of their vision, of their corporate objectives, their decision to focus on core competencies consistent with the tenets of their strategic plan. They remind us of their dedication to best practices, of their unrelenting pursuit of excellence, of their commitment to preservation of the environment. They are also mindful of the need to have in place comprehensive Risk Management and Crisis Management programmes.

Then there's Good Governance and Corporate Social Responsibility to which all Good Corporate Citizens must subscribe. Finally, they remind us that by continued attention to direct and indirect cost management, they will continue to offers customers a superior, value-added package of high-quality service at a competitive price.

This language of the business world and the more general euphemisms that have crept up on us need to be treated with caution. They have been with us in all languages since language itself evolved, but recently their original purpose, that of softening reality and so making it easier to accept, seems to have been taken over by a more sinister one of actually distorting it. And it's the business world again that has been quick to grasp the usefulness of the euphemism in downplaying problems. "Experiencing temporary cash flow difficulties" has long been another way of saying we have no money.

Think for example of that innocuous sounding phrase "collateral damage" that we came to hear so much about during the recent war in Iraq. "Collateral" means something connected to, but aside from, the main subject, and "damage" means loss of something that is desirable. What collateral damage actually means in that military context is the supposedly justifiable killing of non-combatant in the interests of achieving a particular objective

Let's take a few less sinister but still worrying examples of contemporary usage. How about this one from the sensitive world of retailing: Do you know what "shrinkage" means? And it's not what happened to that silk shirt you put in the washing machine! "Shrinkage" is the word used to describe theft—shoplifting that costs the retail industry a great deal of money each year.

Here are a few more. Drug addicts are called "substance abusers", drunks are described as being inebriated, intoxicated, or tipsy. A brothel is called a massage parlour, pornographic shows are frequently referred to as adult entertainment, and prostitutes described variously as bargirls, hostesses, escorts and masseuses. A lie is a fib, a fabrication, a cover story, untruth, inaccuracy.

When we're sick we're indisposed (and in the language of diplomacy that's another lie), and if our children are noisy we probably describe them as boisterous young-sters. The neighbours' children are, of course, always noisy brats. Short people are "vertically challenged" and those that are fat are described as "generously proportioned".

Understandably perhaps, death itself seems to demand many kinds of automatic euphemistic response. "How long has she been gone?" "Did she pass away peace-fully?" Apart from passing away, some people "expire" or "pass on".

In our country at least, as well as this tradition of avoiding telling it as it is, there is now also a curious habit of making sure any charitable contribution to society receives the maximum publicity. Thus we see reports and photos of the managing director of a company against a background of the company's logo, presenting an over-sized cheque to one deserving cause or another. Efforts such as these by companies and business organisations to draw attention to their social contribution activities can often have the effect of provoking cynicism, and if ill-considered, can expose some projects to ridicule.

In an annual report, for instance, one international com-pany, a global leader in its field, detailed its social con-tribution in various countries around the world. It spoke of its awareness of the annual flooding in one Asian country in particular, and the hardship and loss of life this brought to inhabitants of the region. "To counter the effects of this annual flooding and to help people at risk to better prepare themselves, we have instigated a company-sponsored nationwide programme of swimming lessons."

Yes, there it was in black and white, and if I remember correctly, underlined in red. One could just imagine the scene: As the hapless family watch their home and all their belongings being washed away in the raging floodwaters, they are consoled by the voice of the company representative who calls out from a passing boat, "Don't worry, you qualify for free swimming lessons under our nationwide programme."

No doubt the management of most companies, although mindful of the publicity they may gain from their social activities, are sincere enough in wishing to give back to society, to help others. I just wish they wouldn't see the need to draw attention to their efforts.

Telling it as it is in a world of self praise, sanitised truth and what is intended as social politeness, is not always easy. Fortunately it's not always necessary either. It would, for instance, be heartless to say to an acquaintance, or even a close friend who's clearly becoming more obese by the day, "Wow, you're getting fatter and fatter. You must spend all your time eating." Far better to relate to the person with true loving kindness, making no mention of their obvious weight problem. Equally, when a colleague tells you her aunt has passed away you need only offer your condolences, no need to complicate matters by asking non-euphemistically, "When did she die?"

Right Thinking, and Right Speech, avoiding saying things that are hurtful or that might cause embarrassment to others, are mostly quite easy to put into practice. Basically it's simply a matter of saying less. If for instance you don't smoke and someone offers you a cigarette, you need say only, and perhaps with a slight smile, "No, thank you." If you trot out the usual additional, "I don't smoke," you immediately risk being seen as offering an implied and perhaps self-righteous criticism of smokers in general and this one in particular.

Least said the better, especially if you're vertically challenged and you're in a room full of very generously proportioned Sumo wrestlers.

Personality counts

Blending diverse outlooks may be a key
to happiness in work and at home

"She's such a happy person;
nothing seems to put her in a bad mood." "He's always
like that, always miserable, puts everybody in a bad
mood—he must have been born like it." "Oh, he's always
fooling around—never seems to take anything seriously."

When we hear comments such as these about people
we know, perhaps those we work with, we probably
simply accept that we're all different, that we all have a
basic personality. That's the way we are born, probably a
genetic thing, we say, and we justify our reasoning with
comments such as "She takes after her mother in that

respect. The old lady always had a smile on her face, nothing seemed to bother her."

We certainly can't deny that we judge others, categorise them, in terms of their personality. This mental reflex action influences both our social and working lives. If, for instance, we're planning to invite a group of friends to our home for a relaxed get-together we'll almost certainly take into account their various personality types when we're deciding who to invite, and try to achieve some sort of harmonious balance.

It's in the working environment, however, that a person's personality really matters. It might seem obvious, but people are most happy at their work when they're doing something that best matches their personality. This fact has not always been accepted by those in human resource management.

Research over recent years, however, has shown that the link between a person's personality and the degree of satisfaction he or she derives from their work is clearly recognisable and can be predicted. To try to place the whole idea of personality and job satisfaction on a scientific basis, psychologists established a set of five standard personality types which can be broadly described as:

Extroverts: sociable, talkative, friendly and outgoing.

Introverts: quiet, shy, and retiring.

Conscientious: thorough, responsible, diligent.

Emotionally stable: the basically agreeable, cooperative, caring, trusting.

Receptive to ideas: creative, broad-minded, insightful.

Very interestingly, that same research has established that of the five personality types, conscientious people are more likely to perform their jobs efficiently over a long period for a wide range of different types of work. It gets even more interesting, though, when we discover that simply being conscientious won't help if you want to excel as an artist or a musician. If this is where your interests lie, you will certainly need to be the "Receptive to ideas" type with a little bit of the "Extrovert" type thrown in.

Choosing the kind of work we do sometimes seems to happen naturally. "I've always been fascinated by science ever since my school days," says the university researcher. "Farming just comes naturally to me; I guess it's in my blood. I wouldn't do anything else," says another.

There are many other people, however, who are attracted to particular types of work that don't suit their personality, but which they pursue for a variety of reasons. "All my friends work in advertising. It's well paid and you don't have to work too hard," says a trendy-looking young person. "Well, I don't really like having to dress formally every day but my parents wanted me to have a proper job so I'm working for a financial services company. I can't say I enjoy it, but it's a job, and I have to think of the future," says another. Both honest enough comments, and both indicating a mismatch of jobs and personalities.

Understanding what we might call the importance of personality types can help both employers and employees in achieving that desirable state of a happy and productive working environment. Wise employers will take account of personality when interviewing or screening potential job applicants, no doubt placing a high level of importance on their assessment of a candidate's conscientiousness.

For their part, sensible job-seekers will be aware of their own personality type and take this into account when applying for a particular type of job. "OK, the salary seems good and I could probably do the job if I put my mind to it, but could I really accept having to work away from home? And with all the extra study, would I even have time for my music, and what about. . . ?"

Another interesting fact to emerge from the research into personality and its relationship with performance at work, is the degree to which a person's personality type can be used to assess their potential for leadership. We may not all wish to be leaders, but if our personality attributes include extroversion, emotional stability and agreeableness, we can be described as having leadership qualities.

Although the importance of trying to match a person's personality with their type of work is clear enough, the psychologists and researchers may have overlooked another important factor—the opportunity for everyone of us to change.

We may be born with a natural tendency to fit into one of those five personality types, but by following the teachings of the Buddha, especially by practising insightful meditation, we can achieve the inner peace and serenity that comes from understanding. And the joy that understanding can bring will be apparent to all. It will be very much part of our personality, how other people perceive us.

Our personality is, after all, the outward manifestation of our inner thoughts and feelings. It reflects our moods, our likes and dislikes, in effect, what we are.

It would not be reasonable or desirable for everybody to have the same personality—one highly extroverted person in a small group is often enough. What is desirable, though, is for all of us to recognise the importance of tolerance of the many personality types we encounter and often have to deal with on a daily basis.

One of the great joys of successful leadership is the reward of achieving harmony in a group of people with diverse personalities. That harmony not only works for the common good but also can produce results at work.

The medium is the message

**Buddhism teaches that
in seeking the right answers
we must first ask the right questions**

"The 24-hour news channel. We keep you up to date with the latest news from around the world 24 hours a day, every day." Breaking News, Business News, Sports News; it's all there, comprehensive, updated, in-depth coverage. This, as we are constantly reminded, is the Information Age and to drive it we have Information Technology. News is big business. The public's right to know has become the need to know.

The news that we apparently crave by the minute is brought to us by a variety of means that we refer to collectively as the media. Today, television of course dominates, both in terms of immediacy and worldwide coverage. If President George W. Bush stumbles, either literally or verbally, while delivering a speech, millions of people around the world will have viewed the event live via television or seen it repeated as part of that 24-hour news service. We can also catch it on the car radio, have it flashed at us from the Internet, sent as a message via our mobile phone and later of course, we can "read all about it" in the newspapers. "Bush blunders Secret Service steps in. . ."

Isn't this instant access to what's happening in the world something we should exploit to the full? Should we not feel privileged to be living in this Information Age in which we can watch a war taking place thousands of miles away unfold before our eyes? Certainly, we can marvel at the ever-developing technology that makes it possible, but before we become conditioned to seeing the suffering of others as yet another newsworthy event, should we not ask, why do we need to know?

Some of us will be familiar with the life's work and writings of Canadian Marshall McLuhan, a man consi-dered by many to be a leading prophet of the electronic age. It was he in fact who coined the word "media" and later the term "global village". His most well known statement, "The Medium is the Message", was a warn-ing we ignore at our peril.

Much of what McLuhan wrote about was concerned with the effects of advertising and the way the media, in that sense, shapes our lives. News, like advertising, especially if it is manipulated, sends a message. It can strongly influence our views of a particular issue, stir our emotions, even cause us to embark on a specific course of action. Because today, news of every kind is also often instantly analysed from every angle with experts explaining technical aspects and others telling us how it is likely to affect future events, we can too easily lose the motivation to think for ourselves. It's a bit like instant noodles. Just add boiling water, no need to check the ingredients, we know they're good for us—it says so on the packet!

A basic tenet of the Buddha's teachings is that in seeking the right answers we have first to ask the right questions. This is part of what mindfulness means; being aware of the information before us, taking the time to test its veracity, seeking to understand its message.

The news items that are fed to us by the hour and sometimes by the minute are simply snapshots of moments of time. They are there for their moment but we are always part of this moment. Think of how one event, subject of intense media focus and debate, such as the contest for a major presidential election, quickly becomes a non-event once a new president is elected. How often did you flick through the pages of reports on the war in Iraq in the daily newspapers, leaving them unread because the events they referred to had been overtaken by more recent ones? News quickly loses its appeal when we've heard it already.

Why should we have this craving for instant news gratification? Part of the answer, certainly with many young people, is our fascination with technology where the medium is indeed the message. If we know that simply by pressing a button on our mobile phone we can get the latest information on whatever interests us, it's something we feel impelled to do. Another reason is we're constantly being reminded by the purveyors of news that we need to be informed about almost every-thing, with the implication that if we're not up to the minute, on top of the situation, somehow we're not fully equipped to function in today's world.

If a colleague at work suddenly says, "Have you heard the news?" and if we haven't, or don't know what the question refers to, we immediately start to wonder what's happened. Has the company suddenly gone bankrupt, the messenger won the lottery, the boss' wife given birth to twins? An open-ended question like this is almost guaranteed to receive the response, "What news?" Our colleague is using that old trick of playing on our curiosity. Had the question been, "Have you heard the messenger has won over 10 million on the lottery?" its effect would have been different.

It's obvious and perhaps inevitable that more and more, today's news is often managed, either by the media or by those who want to control or influence it. As the media increasingly becomes the message, it's more important than ever that we treat news and information with a questioning mind, prepared to see both sides of an issue, and not jump to conclusions.

Television in particular gives people simultaneous access to any event. In doing so, it clearly diminishes, or destroys altogether, many of the close ties of family life based on oral communication. In its place, it provides a kind of global theatre where people are actors on an electronic stage. It is on this stage that humanity can all too easily be reduced to yet another newsbyte; one which leaves little room for loving kindness and compassion before going over to the White House for an update of the latest events in Washington.

Older workers should be valued

Rising bias against old people not justified
by research or common sense

The traditional respect that
the young are required to show to their seniors has long
been an integral part of Thai culture, inextricably linked
with the core precepts of the Buddha and one that is
universally admired.

Today there are signs, especially in the workplace, that
those values which have guided successive generations
of young people are being threatened by our technologi-
cally-driven and marketing-oriented consumer society in
which traditional skills and values are seen by some young
people as being outmoded and even irrelevant.

"I don't seem to be able to communicate with my children these days," lamented one mother recently. "They spend all their free time sitting in front of the computer. I wouldn't mind so much if they were doing something useful, but all they do is play games and communicate with strangers on one of those chatrooms. Even when their grandparents visit they hardly notice their presence."

The need for young people to develop computer-driven communication skills is obvious enough in the business world where computer literacy is now essential for career development. Although this is to be encouraged, it must not be seen as an end in itself.

There will always be the perception by the young and ultra-fashionable that only they are in touch with what matters. They follow and sometimes create new trends in the way they dress and entertain themselves. This is nothing new; it's always been this way. Their perception that older people are not "with it" and will never understand them is also another fact of the often discussed "generation gap".

The idea that older people are somehow less able to make a useful contribution in terms of performance is one that is shared by many young and not so young managers in business. Older workers are seen as less likely to adapt to new ways of doing things, especially tasks involving computer technology. They are also perceived as likely to be more frequently absent, less trainable, and less committed to their company or profession than some of their younger counterparts. Those who subscribe to this view often justify it with remarks like, "You can't teach an old dog new tricks," and "At a certain age, people begin to lose their memory."

Although they may well still treat older people, especially the very elderly, with the traditional respect that is expected and even demanded by Thai society, they still regard them as not being quite part of their own world, not people with whom they can fully interact.

That commonly held view is, however, not only shortsighted; it is simply wrong. A whole body of scientific research has shown that on the contrary, older people at work are likely to be more committed, are receptive to new ideas, and are less likely to be absent than their younger counterparts. They are more committed, for instance, because they have a strong sense of loyalty and responsibility, and are receptive to new ideas because experience has taught them that the development of wisdom requires an open and curious mind. They are also less likely to take time off than their younger counterparts.

As far as memory loss is concerned, research again shows that this mainly happens with people over the age of 65 who may begin to experience a slight deterioration in their short-term memory. Examples of sharp-minded and energetic individuals who pursue their interests or life's work well past retirement age are everywhere. We all know or have heard of someone who belongs in that category.

Computer games are one area where young people love to show off their considerable skills, often providing amazing displays of dexterity and problem solving; attributes in themselves which can only be admired and which are clearly useful when applied to more serious tasks. When the latest hot game product is launched it's likely to attract a keen and knowledgeable audience of these savvy youngsters, who exchange comments and remarks in the verbal shorthand only they understand.

True to form, when one new and much-awaited game was launched recently at a computer show, a large gathering of these young gamesters was seen milling around the stand, eager to discover what new features the new game promised.

Sample versions had been prepared and were available for customers to try out on a number of the specially prepared play stations. Among the jostling crowd an old man with thick-lensed glasses and walking with a stick was seen peering at one of the computer screens.

Very deliberately he tapped the keyboard and moved the mouse carefully, smiling quietly when the monitor displayed a sudden burst of super realistic animation. "Just take a look at him," one youngster whispered to his friends, "D'you think we ought to show him how it's done?" Their half-joking discussion was interrupted by an announcement from the small group of company officials. "Ladies and gentlemen, before we reveal the amazing features of one of the most exciting computer games available today, I would like to introduce the man whose groundbreaking and innovative technology has made them possible. One of the world's foremost leaders in games technology and designer of. . . ." Making his way to the microphone amidst a burst of applause from the obviously appreciative audience was the old man the youngsters had thought might have needed their help.

This topical story illustrates a curious contradiction in how we regard and value older people. On one hand we readily accept that in many areas of education and professional disciplines those from whom we learn and seek advice such as teachers and doctors will often be in the "old people" category.

We know, too, the maturity and wisdom they have acquired from simply experiencing life can be invaluable sources of inspiration and guidance of benefit to everyone. Yet in the context of the workplace, or in areas considered the preserve of the young, the value and the contribution older workers can make to the success of any business enterprise is often overlooked.

Simply accepting the fact of growing old, even tolerating older people with a sort of benevolent compassion, is not enough. We must appreciate the fact that although they are simply further along the path of life, they share the same moment with all of us.

And if they have the wisdom to live it with joy, wonder, an ever-searching and questioning mind, we can only benefit from their presence.

Agreeing to disagree

**To deal with conflict,
we must first recognise it
and identify its causes**

When we think of conflict we tend to think of a situation where there is strong disagreement or even hostility between individuals or groups of people. Of course, it manifests itself at every level, between governments and the people they represent, between one nation and another, between groups of nations. We all know that when this happens, war with its inevitable consequences can follow.

As individuals, we may not be able to do much to influence conflict between nations. Whatever our views, most of us can only watch as the opposing sides become more and more entrenched in their positions and the diplomatic language becomes more openly antagonistic and combative.

However, conflict in our daily lives, especially when it arises at work, is a different matter. This is something we can do something about. First, we can consciously seek to prevent it, and if it eventually raises its unwelcome head, then with love and understanding we can find a solution.

Have you ever gone to work in an optimistic frame of mind, keen to get on with the project in hand, only to find your usually friendly and enthusiastic colleagues looking morose and sullen? Something is clearly wrong. Perhaps the problem lies with something you have said or done, or it may be related to something or someone else. Your sense conflict may already have occurred, or that it is brewing, and while you are aware of the situation and do not wish to say or do anything to make it worse, you naturally want to know what's going on.

Recognising that conflict exists is the first step in resolving it, and in doing so we often believe we know what causes it, especially when it happens in the work environment. It's all a matter of poor communication, we say; "How can they agree on anything when they hardly talk to one another? Our manager never explains anything properly. How can he expect us to do what he wants?"

These and similar comments are common enough when something does go wrong, but are poor communications really the main culprit? In fact, research shows that while not communicating properly can be a contributing factor in work conflicts, they more often arise from personality clashes and organisational problems.

Personality clashes tend to flare up between people when the underlying differences in peoples' attitudes, character and feelings that are normally kept in check, become polarised by a particular event, which challenges an individual's fundamental thinking. Such fundamental differences can quickly lead to a confrontation, and the seeds of conflict, with others taking sides, are sown.

Conflicts resulting from organisational problems occur because different departments have different priorities. When, for instance, bonus-related production targets are threatened by quality control demands, potential for conflict is high.

How we handle these work-related conflicts can make all the difference between what can be the beginning of a long-running feud and the opportunity to quickly resolve potential problems and clear the air on important issues.

Clearly, each conflict situation demands its own approach, but there are well-proven general rules that we ignore at our peril. There is, for instance, a natural tendency particularly in some non-western cultures to downplay the situation. Managers may try to ignore the obvious signs of trouble with a breezy, "OK, let's move on, folks."

It's important in this context for those of us with managerial responsibility to realise that people with strong opposing views look to us to recognise and identify the nature of a problem and to take the initiative to try to settle the ensuing dispute in a fair and even-handed manner.

The good news here is that there are approaches that work, and perhaps the most effective is the direct approach. This uses the tried and tested techniques of problem-solving where the opposing views are recognised, discussed and analysed in a joint and balanced effort to assess the merits of each, with a conclusion being reached based on consensus and goodwill. This approach is generally successful because it leaves everyone with a sense that the problem has been solved; issues are brought to the surface and dealt with.

Another technique, the bargaining approach, works when both parties have ideas towards a solution but cannot find common ground. The focus here is on finding a compromise. There is a price to pay, however, because compromise is just that—it involves give and take, and no one may be completely satisfied.

The "OK, let's look at the problem, discuss the merits of both points of view, then I'll make the decision because I'm the boss," method will work, as the problem gets resolved. However, it is a method that should only be used when neither of the first two approaches results in a solution. It is likely that the person whose views are overridden may harbour resentment, and for the sake of future harmony that individual may have to be continually appeased.

Finally, conflict can sometimes be resolved by an appeal to the good sense of those involved. "It's really not worth arguing about, and certainly not worth jeopardising our friendly, cooperative working relationships. After all, we are trying to achieve the same ends. It's simply how we should achieve those ends that we arguing about."

When conflict arises between people it is often seen as a negative force, one that promotes ill feeling, anger and resentment. It can, however, trigger a natural process of cleansing and healing. To deal with conflict we must first recognise it and identify its causes. We need to look deep within ourselves where the seeds of anger and intolerance lie dormant. When these are exposed to the pure light of Dhamma, they are put to flight.

True colours

**First impressions count,
but they can also be very misleading**

The young man was in his early 20s and his mother noticed he had spent most of the afternoon getting ready for another evening out with his girlfriend. This was in marked contrast to the usual " 'Bye Mum, we're going out to eat with some friends, won't be back till late, see you!"

On those occasions, getting ready meant a quick shower, a change from one set of casual clothes to another, a check of the fashionable "Fido Dido" hairstyle, and perhaps a few gulps of fruit juice. All that was left to be done was to muster a cheeky reassuring smile and he was gone, leaving Mum to shake her head in bemused resignation.

This day, though, was different. When he finally emerged, maternal resignation turned into wide-eyed amazement. Now "de-spiked", his hair was slicked back, giving him a mature, sober look, and together with a neat shirt and tie and well pressed trousers, he looked like everyone's idea of a well-dressed young man. Trying to adjust to this remarkable transformation, Mum naturally wanted to know where her remodelled son was going. "Oh, Porntip's introducing me to her parents for the first time."

Then, flashing that trademark cheeky smile, he added, "Got to create a good first impression."

The idea that first impressions count is one we have heard since childhood; and like the young man about to meet his possible future in-laws, we tend to take it seriously and generally make a special effort to present ourselves in the best possible light when we're likely to be judged by others.

Although scientific research confirms that first impressions do indeed count, we need to remind ourselves that this process works both ways. Whenever we meet people for the first time, just as we are forming that all-important initial impression, whether we realise it or not, they too are evaluating us.

In fact, that same research demonstrated that an initial impression, based upon appearance and demeanour, is created in the first 60 seconds, and when we start speaking to one another a final impression is formed based on what is said during the next 45 to 60 minutes. Perhaps, though, the most important finding of this research is that once that first impression is formed, neither party changes their opinion quickly or easily.

The part that Right Thinking, Right Speech, and Right Action play in this introductory process can be clearly seen when we also learn that in those first few minutes impressions are formed by body language (70 per cent), tone of voice (20 per cent), and what we say (10 per cent).

First impressions, then, play a vital role in how we relate to one another; and because of this, especially when we are judging other people, we need to look beyond the attractive physical appearance and the pleasing words.

People trying to impress others, especially in a job interview, will often present themselves in a way which they believe will suit a particular situation. Moreover, those strong first impressions can often be way off the mark, and a rush to judgment can lead to problems later on.

Consider also the fact that in most relationships between married couples for instance, initial impressions formed under the heady mixture of romance and lust tend to change, sometimes dramatically, over time. Ordinary friendships too are often broken when one person sees the other in an entirely new light.

The folly of relying on first impressions is brought into sharp focus when, for instance, a formerly respected public figure is caught out betraying a scandalous and hitherto unrevealed aspect of his character. We may have seen him on television or even met him personally, and in that first-impression moment we may have believed what he said and how he said it, because that was what we wanted to hear. We were taken in by the pleasing physical appearance, the carefully judged body language, the well-chosen words and the gentle, modulated voice. When we see the real character of that person exposed, we find it hard to accept. "I just can't believe it," is a common reaction on these occasions.

How we judge other people in those first few moments when we meet them for the first time will depend largely on our own values. The most successful journalists and professional television interviewers know that by being open, non-judgmental, and asking questions in a relaxed, conversational style, they can encourage the person being interviewed to open up, often revealing heartfelt emotions that would be difficult to fake. People who quickly respond to one another in this way do so because a sense of mutual trust is firmly established in those "first-impression" moments.

Whether we are dressed in our best "meet the public" attire or wearing our favourite "hanging around the house" clothes, the impression we convey to others when meeting them for the first time can always be the same if we demonstrate tolerance, understanding, respect and humility. If we are open and straightforward with everybody with whom we come in contact, their immediate impression of us will be based on what we truly are. In that same spirit, their response will also more accurately reflect their true nature.

Presenting ourselves as we are is especially important at work when we are likely to encounter first-impression situations on a regular basis.

If physical appearance, enhanced by expensive clothes, is important to us then those factors will clearly influence our initial assessment. If we are wise to take the time to base our judgment on less superficial factors, we will discover the true nature of people we work with or meet in a business environment, and with whom we must establish a relationship based on mutual trust and respect.

By the way, what were your first impressions when you began to read this *Dhamma Moments*? If they were favourable, you will have continued reading up to this point, demonstrating yet again that the more we are impressed with what we see at first glance, the more we will want to know.

Dhamma moments in daily life

The road to nowhere

Compassion and understanding
can overcome fear, anger and envy

Remember those first gnaw-
ing pains of childhood toothache? "Just forget about it
and it will go away," we might have been told by well-
meaning friends or even parents. Of course the pain didn't
go away, although when we became occupied it might
have faded, but it was still there, and eventually the bad
tooth had to come out.

Isn't this the way many of us behave even as adults
when something unpleasant or worrying occurs in our
lives? We try to forget about it, hoping it will go away.
And the more we try to ignore it, the worse it becomes.

It's the same with our emotions, especially those negative feelings and responses such as anger, fear and jealousy. We've all experienced them, and most of us still do, but how we deal with them makes all the difference. Let's take a closer look. We'll start with anger.

"Don't get mad, get even." Most of us have heard that slick comment, but we know that's not the answer. The first thing we must do is to drop the get-even bit, then we're halfway there.

In Buddhism, anger is classified as an unskilled state of mind. This is very important, and it is crucial to see that there are no exceptions. Buddhism allows no place for "righteous anger". In other words, there is no conceivable case where anger is justifiable or where it is the most appropriate response.

This might be hard to accept. It's easy to think of many examples of real grievances and injustices that would seem to justify anger. But whatever the situation, an angry response is not right. When we're angry we can't think clearly, and we may well say or do something we will regret. Whichever way we look at it, getting angry will only make the situation worse. Being mindful of anger is the first step. Think of it as a poison. Applying the antidote of loving kindness is the next step.

If you're driving on the expressway and some aggressive driver cuts in on you, you have a choice. You can allow your anger to flare up, flash your lights, rant and rave, or immediately cut it off with a thought of loving kindness, "I hope he gets home to his family safely." Try it, it works.

Can we do the same with fear? Well, like anger we must recognise it for what it is—a physical and emotional anxiety about something known or unknown over which we have no control. And often it's the unknown which causes us the greatest fear.

Fear is always within ourselves, it's there because we allow it to overcome our rational thought. Being mindful of fear in all its forms will allow us to deal with this very basic emotion without which many creatures would not survive. Think of the classic "fear, fright, and flight" reaction of animals, including humans, and which in our case can cause us to jump out of the path of sudden danger.

But fear can often be destructive unless we tackle it head on. And when we do, the fears we have nursed, and which have caused us so much anxiety, often turn out to be groundless.

Let's take a simple example. Your boss at work is especially keen on "team spirit"; he expects everyone to play their part, and has precious little time for shirkers. He's planned a big charity event for a weekend which clashes with a close friend's wedding. You want to tell him you can't make it, but are scared of his reaction. You feel that not taking part might even affect your chances of promotion. You consider making up an excuse after the event, but that would mean lying. As preparations for the charity get under way, you feel trapped. Your fear factor increases.

Finally you overcome your fear and tell him about having to attend your friend's wedding. "That's wonderful," he says, "I love weddings and wish I could be there with you, but as you know, we have this charity event to take care of. I remember meeting your friend at that sports day last year; please give her my best wishes."

Even in situations where our fears are justified, allowing fear itself to take over will only make a bad situation worse. Staying calm and thinking rationally will often save the day.

Applying this approach to dealing with jealousy may seem to be completely unworkable. Jealousy and its close ally, envy, can be even more difficult to conquer than anger or fear, both of which are usually short-lived. But jealousy and envy can exist for as long as we permit them, and while they do, they can be especially destructive.

The first thing we must accept about jealousy and envy is that they lead nowhere. Being envious of someone else's achievements or possessions will not bring them to us. In fact while we harbour these negative emotions we are less able to get on with our own lives. Our situation is likely to get worse, creating a negative cycle of events. So how do we deal with this emotion, often described as a green-eyed monster? The answer again is simply loving kindness.

By substituting loving kindness for envy when, for instance, we hear of someone else's success, we can feel joy on their behalf. When a loved one gives us cause to feel hurt, left out, jealous in fact, we can in a spirit of loving kindness know that we have no cause to fear if our love is true.

Anger, fear, jealousy are in us only with our permission. Replace them instead with consciousness, loving kindness, compassion and understanding, and they simply won't exist.

Beyond sight and sound

**The evidence of the impermanence
of our material world is there for all to see;
the only constant is change itself**

There's a very old dog in the compound where friends of mine live. Their house is fairly old and set in a corner, and looks onto trees and greenery that is home to birds, squirrels, and the occasional cat. "We really love it here," they say, almost every time I pay them a visit. "We know we're in the city, but this little bit of nature is so relaxing, almost inspiring."

Most days, the old dog, too, makes its rounds of the garden. It's completely blind and deaf, but it seems to have retained its sense of smell which it uses like an olfactory radar as it shuffles and bumps around.

When I first saw this old family pet I wondered why it had not been put to sleep by the owners. Surely, I thought, it would be kinder, more humane.

On a recent visit one of the owners, a family doctor, was in the garden, and as I looked compassionately at the glazed eyes of the old dog, he seemed to anticipate my question. "We decided we have no right to end its life, you know; it's strange, but in its own way it copes very well. It recognises all the familiar smells and seems almost content in its own world."

As we spoke, the handicapped animal lumbered slowly to its feet and as we watched it shuffle away, its nose close to the ground like a bloodhound, I tried to imagine how I would cope with being blind and deaf. The more I thought about it, the more awful it seemed.

Imagine it for yourself. First, the complete darkness that only the blind can know, and the total absence of sound that produces a silence which is beyond silence. I sat down on one of the garden seats near my friend's house. The afternoon sunlight dappled the ground through the trees, two squirrels performed their arboreal acrobatics, and there was the twittering and tweeting of birds. I could see and hear, at least with my eyes and ears.

There in the distance was the dog; tired perhaps from its rounds, it appeared to be sleeping in its favourite shady spot. Was it dreaming, I wondered? And if it was, could it see and hear in its dreams, just as we do when we enter that mysterious and colourful world? In our dreams, sounds and sights are all around us even though our eyes are closed and our ears are deaf to the outside world.

The 19th-century American poet, Henry David Thoreau, wrote, "I hear beyond the range of sound. I see beyond the verge of sight. I see, smell, taste, hear, feel that everlasting something to which we are all allied at once."

Isn't that how we see when we practise mindfulness? In particular, when we practise meditation? At first we are blind, then we learn to see with an ever increasing clarity. We are deaf, but as we progress with our meditation we learn to hear the very whisperings of our mind.

Suddenly I viewed the dog with great respect. The doctor was absolutely right; it did seem content with its lot, and appeared to know its place in the order of things. And the dog seemed to be a perfect example of mindfulness. An inspiration to me to be more mindful. By using its remaining senses of touch and smell, it was able to navigate its world, a world whose smells and textures change constantly, stimulating the old dog to follow its exploring instincts. To live yet, in spite of the darkness and the silence.

When we are blessed with the health and vitality of youth, we usually aren't yet wise enough to understand that it won't last forever. Not even for more than a few years. In our folly we tend to believe that we are the exception. We will never end up like the old dog, and even if we ever did, we would rather die, we say, than live like that.

Well, now we know better. The evidence of the impermanence of our material world is here for all to see, from our own ever-fading youth to the once familiar objects of our world, being no more. Nothing ever stays the same. The only constant is change itself.

A few days later, thoughts of the old dog came back into my mind as I was busy in my office. A phone call, then an email to deal with, but I let the thoughts stay, and then in a quiet moment I visualised the sniffing, shuffling animal as it made its way around the garden. I also recalled the trees and the greenery, the leaping squirrels and sounds of the birds, and wished I had the power to let the dog see and hear again.

Meanwhile I resolved to be yet more mindful. Mindful of the world we see but can't hear, of which we hear but can't see.

Nothing is what it seems

Viewing the world as an illusion
can be a surprisingly powerful means
to discover the true and joyful nature
of the Dhamma in ourselves

When I was studying over-seas, I lived for a while in my own apartment, and perhaps in the folly of youth, decided to brighten up my bathroom. I chose yellow for the walls—in fact I remember the label on the can, "Sunshine Yellow".

I set about my task with enthusiasm, imagining how my small bathroom would look with its new coat of paint, and wishing I was more skilful as a painter and decorator. Fortunately I had carefully laid old newspapers to catch the drips, and as I progressed, learning not to load the brush with too much paint, I was able to put most of the "Sunshine Yellow" where it was supposed to go—on the walls.

Finally, late in the afternoon, the job was done. My hands were a mess, the brush looked like a yellow lollipop, but the newspapers had done their job, and as I cleaned up I sang my own version of that lovely whimsical Beatles hit, "We all splash in our yellow bath-a-room, yellow bath-a-room, yellow bath-a-room. . . ."

Pleased with my efforts and my choice of "Sunshine Yellow", I surveyed my work with youthful pride, and right on cue, the sun beamed through the frosted-glass window. Time to get on with my studies, I told myself, I couldn't live in the bathroom, however bright and cheerful it was. And then, to my dismay, I spotted two large blobs of yellow paint on the bathtub. It was made from the newly fashionable acrylic, plastic-like material, and I knew removing the yellow smears without damaging the surface would be difficult. I would have to be very careful. I couldn't use any type of solvent. Hot water, perhaps that would do the trick. A few minutes later I tried this approach using a rag dipped in a bowl of hot soapy water. With small circular movements I tackled the first spot.

No effect. If anything the paint seemed to have been absorbed into the surface of the acrylic material, and appeared even to be increasing in size after my efforts with the hot cloth.

I began to be anxious. My rental agreement with the landlord stipulated that I would be held responsible for any damage to furnishing and fittings and I could hardly afford to pay for a new bathtub. I decided to seek advice, and called a fellow student who was majoring in industrial chemistry—perhaps he could come up with something that would work. His comments, though, were far from encouraging. "If the paint has been absorbed into the outer surface of the bathtub, anything you do to try to remove it will only make things worse," he said, adding, "Why don't you just paint the whole tub yellow?" I told him that wasn't very funny, and decided to put it out of my mind and went to close the bathroom door as a sort of symbolic gesture.

The sun no longer shone through the window but the yellow walls had certainly transformed my "bath-a-room". What a pity about the bathtub, I thought. If only I had covered it completely, I sighed, glancing once more at those offending yellow stains, and turned to close the door.

I paused and took another look. Where were they? I couldn't see those yellow marks. I peered closely. They had completely disappeared. Just then the sun cast a late afternoon beam through the glass, this time the light dappled the floor, spotting the dark tiles with yellow blobs of fading sunlight. Yes, I had actually been trying to remove spots of light from the tub! How could I have been so stupid? They must have moved slightly while I was desperately trying to remove them. And I didn't even notice.

Of course, when I related this story to my friends it caused much merriment and mirth, especially when the sun shone through the classroom windows. But later in life, as I learned more and more about Buddhism, it also became an important lesson on the illusory nature of what we may believe is real.

Is this material and physical world the true reality? Or is it all an illusion? Does it exist only in our minds? A young novice monk, observing a flag blowing in the wind, asked a fellow monk, "Is it the wind that moves the flag, or the flag that moves the wind?" The answer, that it was the wind blowing on the flag that caused it to move, seemed obvious. But the young monk was not satisfied; he saw it in a different context and believed that the moving flag must, in turn, influence the wind. They turned to the abbot for an answer. "It is neither. Mind is moving," he said.

Understanding that reality exists only in what we commonly refer to as our mind—which itself is simply a means of communicating with a greater cosmic consciousness—is a first step to true contentment. As we strive to loosen the bonds of desire and the unhappiness they inevitably bring, the acceptance of the physical world as an illusion allows us to become truly fearless and relaxed in our life. We can accept things and people as they are, or as they seem to be. We can take life as it comes, finding something of value in everything, even in suffering itself.

One of the subjects I took as a student was art, and especially after my yellow bathroom experience, I soon realised that reality—colour, for instance—disappears as light fades. All shapes and colours, being products of light, appear to vanish with the onset of night. Then there are the many tricks used in drawing and painting that rely on creating an illusion of dimension and texture, and even of light and shadow.

Eventually I asked myself, "How is reality any different from a dream? And if it isn't possible to perceive any substantial difference between the two, why bother to believe there is a difference?"

Viewing the world from this standpoint, that it is an illusion, can be a surprisingly powerful means to discover the true and joyful nature of the Dhamma in ourselves. We know that whatever colour we paint our walls, it is only there in our mind's eye.

Animal virtues

All living creatures deserve
our loving kindness and compassion

I am not a great watcher of television. I find most of the programmes neither entertaining nor interesting, and while like most of us, I feel the need to keep up with the news, these days I brace myself each time I turn to the news channel, afraid of seeing yet another report of a tragic event.

There are, however, certain programmes that do get my appreciative attention. Often beautifully and skilfully filmed, they can have all the poignancy of a great tragic drama, the fascination of an unravelling mystery thriller, or provide the inspiration of a heroic tale. I have watched births that take place under the most amazing circumstances, and battles between bitter enemies. And I have seen some of the extraordinary strategies and methods evolved by living creatures and plants to ensure their continuing survival.

Yes, it's those wonderful wildlife programmes I'm enthusiastic about, though I sometimes think if I see that same cheetah chasing, and finally catching, that poor Thomson gazelle one more time, I too will take off at more than 70 miles an hour!

And I'm not in favour of what seems to be a recent trend for humans to get in on the act. It's the other living creatures which fascinate and inspire me. Give me the quiet narrative of a genuine naturalist and let the animals, insects, birds and fish speak for them.

For me, their world is one great symphony of birth, life, death and rebirth. A world whose myriad creatures in their infinite variety have evolved to play their specialised part in a natural, interdependent system. And it is a world where these same creatures display what can only be described as virtue.

It has been said by a leading natural history professor that animals may not be ethical, but they are often virtuous. Can animals actually display virtue? We have to accept that what is termed ethical behaviour as defined in the Five Precepts is confined to humans, but in the higher animals at least, there are so many examples of virtuous behaviour that we must accept its existence. We have all heard of the acts of domestic animals, especially those by the family dog, that can only have been motivated by a sense of virtue. I even remember reading of a wild monkey in India which jumped into a river to rescue a human baby. Was this an instinctive maternal act? Did the monkey mistake the human child for one of its own offspring? Whatever the cause or motivation, the act itself was undoubtedly virtuous.

We are constantly being reminded by scientists that we meddle in the natural world at our peril. Sadly, when we do, the wildlife also suffers, driven sometimes into extinction by the excesses and self-serving interests of humans. I was particularly saddened when one of the Animal World programmes recently included images of racks of elephant tusks. Here in Thailand the elephant is an integral part of our cultural heritage, yet we can all see the sad sight of these great beasts being used in our cities as a means to generate income for their human caretakers, the mahouts. We remind ourselves that from the mighty elephant to the tiny ant, all living creatures deserve our loving kindness and compassion. All of the higher animals can distinguish between a non-caring attitude and kindness, between compassion and cruelty.

We know of course that by their genetically determined nature, which is programmed to ensure their survival, animals, especially wild ones, can be fierce and apparently cruel. They literally devour their prey, sometimes in a sickening and horrific manner, until they too fall victim to a bigger and even more voracious hunter. Such is the way of the natural world.

From the Buddhist point of view, this apparently cruel and abhorrent behaviour is understood, and its primary purpose—of ensuring survival—is also accepted as being part of the cycle of life and death. As Buddhists we don't ask, "Why did God create all those obnoxious, dangerous, disease-spreading animals?" Flies, mosquitoes and cock-roaches are all part of the same world as the adorable kitten and the faithful family dog.

So if we accept that animals can be virtuous, does this also mean that although they have no sense of morality, or even any need for it, they can be subject to karma? The answer must surely be that because Buddhism sees all life from the perspective of infinity, the cycle of birth and rebirth has always existed. The karmic record of every living being extends also to infinity, and each being has a potential of karma, both good and bad. Because of their lack of moral values, animals can be said to be subjected to karma passively.

I was discussing this question of Buddhism and animals recently with an American friend who lives here with her family and who follows Buddhist principles. After a fairly serious and at times weighty discussion, she recalled a story about one of her friends, whom I'll call Liz, who worked in a pet shop.

Pets have to be fed, and while some animals eat pet food, some eat other animals. Mice are feeder animals and are sometimes sold as such by pet shops.

Liz liked almost everything about working in the pet shop except when she had to sell mice as feeders. But she was an intelligent woman, and she quickly found a true Buddhist solution. Whenever anyone wanted to buy the mice, she asked if they were for pets or feeders. If the person answered "feeder", she chanted "Nam-myohorenge-kyo" three times to the mice so they could have a better life next time.

One day a customer came in and bought some mice from another assistant who had taken over from Liz during her break. Seeing the customer about to pay for them, Liz asked, "Excuse me, are they for pets or feeders?" "Feeders," answered the customer, adding, "and please don't pray over them, the last three I bought that were prayed over got away!"

The sound of silence

When we see or hear things as they really are, acceptance comes naturally

The negative side of the ubiquitous cell phone was brought to my attention one day in a well written and clearly heartfelt plea by a newspaper columnist. And there was also a bitter condemnation, in a letter to the same newspaper, of the excessive noise level from the night market near Lumpini Park.

Just two of the long list of some people's thoughtless and plainly selfish acts. We can all add to this list—the street vendors obstructing the pavements with their carts and stalls, the motorcycle taxi riders monopolising the pavements, and salespeople of all kinds loudly advertising their products.

Apart from complaining, as individuals there's little we can do. Noise is all pervasive in our cities, and this seems especially so in Bangkok. Shopping malls, those great caverns of cacophony, assault our eardrums with a deluge of decibels, department stores, even government offices and banks, all contribute to this most distracting and even debilitating form of pollution.

Noise, then, as it affects those close to it, can certainly be regarded as a form of suffering, an example of the First Noble Truth and our need to be free from its torment, a consequence of craving as pointed out by the Second Noble Truth. At this point, it's logical to ask, if we have no control over it, how can we be free from the noise, thus achieving the state of the Third Noble Truth—the cessation of suffering? I recall asking a similar question to one of my Vipassana meditation teachers when I first discovered the life-changing potential of insight meditation.

The small meditation centre was housed in a sort of garden pavilion in the grounds of a large old house that had so far defied the then highrise building boom. Sadly, at the time of my weekly visits, construction on an adjacent site was often in full swing.

Seeing my pained expression when on my very first visit the noise from the site burst in with a vengeance, the meditation teacher asked what I thought was an odd question. "Does it bother you? The noise, does it upset you? Does it spoil your concentration?"

"Yes, it does. I find it most disturbing. It's also annoying. It's beginning to make me angry. After all, don't we need a quiet place in which to concentrate?" "Yes, but the quiet place is within us. The noise which you find so distracting is external. It only exists if you want it to," the teacher explained.

My expression now showed puzzlement, and seeing this, the teacher motioned to our small group to gather around.

"If we approach meditation from a selfish point of view with the ambition of achieving perfect silence, all noise will become our enemy. When we think like that, we become very emotional, and then where is our meditation? If we notice that we are becoming short-tempered, we should know that we are meditating in a wrong way. Never allow yourself to meditate like that!

"Noise is a challenge. If we can make it part of our meditation, we will make real progress. If we can do this, we will feel confident that we can literally meditate in the middle of traffic. Noise will no longer bother us," he said.

He went on, "While meditating, some people get disturbed by what they see. They close their eyes in order not to see what is in front of them, but then something else will start disturbing them. Meditation should not be an excuse to blame something or somebody for taking away our inner peace. If we accept everything that comes our way, nothing can bother us any more, and our inner peace is there all the time. The point is that whatever obstacle arises as we meditate, if we blame that for our not finding inner peace, then eventually every object becomes our enemy."

When I began meditating, I had a comfortable house next to a monastery. Everything was perfect for practice. A few weeks after I arrived, however, the monastery decided to start a major building project right next to my house. The whole area became a building site, full of heavy machinery, so my whole house was shaking. I felt that my retreat was ruined. It gave me so much trouble I could hardly meditate. I finally complained to my teacher, and he said something that really helped me. The noise, he said, is your meditation. You must make it your friend.

"How can we do that?" I asked. "Right now I feel irritated. In fact, I'm trying to eliminate the noise from my consciousness, but I can't."

To begin with, he said, you have to see suffering in its entirety before you can see your way out of it. Right now, you have a craving for the workmen to stop. There is already aversion in your mind. Suppose you were in the midst of doing something that was very important to you. This aversion could easily flare up into anger, hatred, or even violence. Aversion is already a stressful state. Anger, hatred and violence bring on even greater stress and suffering, both to oneself and to others. But we are not aware of this aversion and suffering, we are in an unwakened state (avija). We blame our dukkha on someone or something else.

Smilingly gently, the teacher then asked me to think about the noise that was annoying me in a calm manner. Still smiling, he inquired, "What happens to the annoyance?"

"When I become aware of the annoyance, it sort of lessens," I replied.

"As soon as you become aware of the annoyance, the aversion fades away. It resolves in the mind. Is it still there?" he asked.

"You mean the annoyance? It's much less. It is still there but it is much less now," I conceded.

It was true. Simply by thinking of it in that way the noise had faded, and with it, my annoyance. The issue was not the noise; it was my reaction to it. We can see that it is possible to break the cycle of suffering by merely looking into our own state of mind. The act of mindfulness is a transcending act. We see things as they are. When we see or hear things as they really are, acceptance comes naturally.

A powerful force for change

Integrating loving kindness and compassion
into our everyday lives

A Western visitor to a Thai temple, the author of many books on cuisine from around the world, took the opportunity to ask an elderly monk a question on the relative merits of the world's cuisine from a Buddhist perspective. "Tell me," she asked, "of all the world's many dishes, which do you think is the most delicious?" "That which is served with loving kindness," smiled the monk. A lesson for the food writer and for each one of us.

Food of course can be both for the body and the mind, but however nutritious it may be, if it is offered begrudgingly or in an unpleasant, negative atmosphere, we won't find it appealing and will either not accept it or do so in sufferance.

Hand in hand with loving kindness is compassion. Just as our mind and body are interdependent, so too these most basic of human qualities are intertwined, and immensely significant. They should form the very core of our thinking, of how we behave towards others, of how we regard ourselves.

But all the loving kindness and all the compassion in the world will do little to help others unless we integrate these qualities into our daily lives. Merely paying lip service to the notion of doing good by occasional and often very public acts of charity will do nothing to benefit others or ourselves. These very positive qualities, although gentle and loving in nature, are in fact, a powerful force for change. Anger and vengeful thoughts and actions can melt under their influence. Hatred itself can turn to love, envy to respect.

A distraught young girl once sought the advice of the wise old man of the village.

"Please, you have to help me," she said. "My grandmother is such a wicked woman. She seems to hate me and does everything to make my life miserable. She seems jealous because I am not old and wrinkled like her and can still dance and sing. I try to please her but nothing I do makes any difference. I cannot stand it any longer. If she died I would not be unhappy."

"Well, it seems she is resentful of your youth and beauty. Her attitude will only get worse, so I will give you this special lotion. It is very powerful but you must apply it gradually," counselled the old man. "After a time changes will take place, your oppressor will be gone and your troubles will be over," he added, and patted the girl on the shoulder. "Go on, take it, but remember you have to rub it in slowly, and do it every day."

Although at first the girl had no thoughts in her mind of attempting anything so drastic as slowly poisoning her tormentor, she had become desperate, and accepted the lotion.

The very next day, pretending to show concern for her grandmother's aches and pains, she persuaded the old lady to let her massage her, gently rubbing in the secret lotion. Knowing she had to be patient, the girl put up with the sarcasm and ungratefulness of her grandmother and persevered with the daily massage sessions.

One day when the lotion was down to the last few drops, to her surprise her grandmother took her hand. "You know, my dear, you are not such a bad girl. I think I have misjudged you. After all, you are my granddaughter. Let's start again, I think we can be friends, don't you?"

Responding in tears to this sudden change of heart, the girl realised she did not want to lose her grandmother after all, and raced back to the old man. "You must do something quickly. I did what you told me, but she has changed, and well, now we love each other and I don't want to lose her. You must give me something to save her." He took her hands in his and smiled a knowing, old-man smile "You have already saved her by your act of loving kindness. Your tormentor has gone, as I said she would, and your troubles are over."

To put loving kindness and compassion into practice as a living expression of Dhamma, we must first love ourselves. With loving kindness within, we can transcend anger and hatred, which cannot coexist with gentleness and compassion.

How often do we become consumed with anger by what we perceive as somebody's unacceptable behaviour? A colleague at work, a noisy, aggressive neighbour, and especially in this city of ill-disciplined and thought-less road users, the daily examples that abound on the city's streets and even pavements.

We may not be able to change the world, but with loving kindness and compassion we can dissipate our anger and in the spirit and practice of Dhamma begin to understand the human condition.

Lazy excuses

Reaping the mental, physical and
spiritual rewards of a job well done

"Do not deceive yourself with laziness, which thinks to practise tomorrow or the next day, or you will die praying for help. Quickly, quickly help yourself and take the essence of truth."—His Holiness the Seventh Dalai Lama, from the *Songs of Spiritual Change*.

Most of us will admit that some of the time we are guilty of that tempting vice of laziness. Often it's in the form of putting off a job that needs doing in the morning, to the afternoon. Then we tell ourselves we'll do it after dinner. Spurred by guilt, we make another attempt to tackle it, but by now we feel too sleepy, and the task remains unfinished.

His Holiness the 14th Dalai Lama outlines three types of laziness, each easy to recognise and each of which most of us are guilty of. They are the laziness of indolence, leading to procrastination described above; the laziness of inferiority—doubting your abilities: "I could never learn to do that, I'm just no good with computers," and the third type of laziness, often seen in young people today, the laziness of attachment to negative actions, mindless pleasures, as seen in today's obsessive interest in computer games.

I sometimes come across what I call pre-emptive laziness from friends or colleagues when I ask, for instance, "Are you going anywhere near the post office on your travels?" "I'm afraid not, I'll be tied up all morning," they reply. Believing I'm about to ask them some favour which might involve them in a minor inconvenience, they immediately pre-empt any further questions such as, "Would you mind posting this letter for me, it's already stamped?"

These days, becoming overweight is a major problem for many people around the world, and children are not exempt. Estimates show that here in Thailand around 14 per cent of children of school age are overweight. Yes, they eat too much of the wrong type of food, but according to the research, a major reason for their being overweight is their lack of physical exercise and their preference for lolling around watching television or playing computer games.

The type of laziness which can lead to obesity and all the associated medical problems it brings is particularly insidious. The more we avoid exercise, the fatter and lazier we become—it's a self-perpetuating cycle of cause and effect.

When we're feeling particularly lazy, we probably ask ourselves, "So what's wrong with my taking it easy for a change? I've worked hard all week. I reckon I deserve a break, why shouldn't I put my feet up?" The answer is clear enough of course, and it's in the question. If we really are simply taking a well deserved break we would not be prompted by guilt to justify our laziness in disguise, even to ourselves. We probably know there's some outstanding job we must finish. Our well deserved break is simply yet another excuse for procrastination. We must finish the job first to earn that well deserved break.

Recognising laziness is one thing. But how do we avoid it? How do we break its self-perpetuating grip on our lives?

In practising mindfulness we think about every aspect of our being, and of the world surrounding us. And in confronting laziness and sloth, we also practise mindfulness. We can do it when carrying out the most simple everyday household tasks and in the more complicated routines of our workaday life. Whatever the task is, we must approach it in a mindful way, remembering everything we do is of the moment, and resolve to do it methodically and thoroughly and not to be diverted by sensual distractions. If it's a report we are trying to finish before lunchtime, then we must try to do our best to finish it. If it's something that requires a greater deal of effort on our part to do well, and the sacrifice of our leisure time, then we must make the effort and sacrifice our leisure.

Does this mean that we have to be workaholics in order not to be lazy? To devote ourselves to our work with no regard to leisure time? Fortunately we all know that is not the case.

What we may not fully realise, however, is that by not being lazy in every sense of the word will bring enormous benefits to ourselves and to the lives of others.

On a very practical level our bodies will benefit from the effort of walking instead of taking the car to the local shop, of cleaning out the spare room this weekend instead of at some indefinite time in the future. Mentally we will be free of that gnawing guilt that never lets up. And spiritually we will have taken an important step along the path of Dhamma.

LAZY EXCUSES

Lessons in humility

**Only by being truly humble
can we achieve
the perfection we seek in life**

The more ripe a clump of rice becomes on a growing rice plant, the lower it bows down its head.

As we progress through the many stages of our lives, many of us believe that becoming good—in the sense of being virtuous, kind and considerate to others, honest and open in our relationships, forgiving and tolerant of the perceived transgressions of others, charitable to those less fortunate than ourselves, at least in the material sense—is our ultimate goal in life. But we must learn that achieving all those virtues we believe constitute goodness is not enough. Our ultimate goal in this life must be to become humble. Only then can we achieve the greatest happiness and joy.

Becoming truly humble, as we all know, seems sometimes almost impossible. In our daily lives we are confronted with situations where we believe our skills and knowledge are often superior to those of the people around us. We watch them struggle with a particular task and feel we want to take over and show them how it's done. But there's always something they can do better than we can, and when that happens, it's our turn to be humble.

Some years ago, in the early 1930s, a young European girl, a talented musician and a budding concert pianist, was visiting Bonn in Germany, the quiet university town and the birthplace of Ludwig van Beethoven. Naturally, Beethoven's house, by then a well preserved museum, was to be the highlight of her visit. Accustomed to the admiration of her peers and the praise of music critics in her own country, she felt somehow superior to the other visitors who, like her, were being shepherded around the house.

And suddenly there it was: A piano, once used by Beethoven, still gleaming in its polished beauty, with its lid open as if waiting for the master to create his musical magic. She could not resist. She sat down on the padded stool and with quiet confidence began to play a short but well known piece. A burst of subdued applause from the other visitors greeted her impromptu performance. Feigning modesty with phrases such as "Well, I do play a little in my own country," she was thrilled with the reaction. Her feeling of superiority now seemed even more justified.

Just then a slightly frail, elderly man had quietly come into the room and he too was now seated at the piano. But he simply sat there, almost as if in meditation.

Another visitor in the group came over and whispered in her ear, "Do you know who that old man is?" She had no idea, and shook her head. "That's Paderewski, the Polish pianist, probably one of the greatest in the world today."

Hardly able to control her excitement, the girl watched as the old man still sat quietly at the piano, saying and doing nothing. She decided she had at least to take the opportunity to speak to such a world famous pianist. But when, she wondered, would he begin to play? Finally she approached him.

"Mr Paderewski, aren't you going to play? It would be a great honour for us." "No, young lady, I am not going to play. In fact I am not worthy to play on this piano. I can only respect it." "I am sorry, Mr Paderewski, I don't understand." The old man turned, admonishing her with his eyes, "This, young lady, is the piano of Beethoven, my teacher. I am nothing before this piano, before my teacher, I am totally worthless. I am not worthy even to touch it." When she listened to his words, she was deeply moved. It was the beginning of her own humility.

The girl was at the growing, the developing stage of her life. She had respect for Beethoven, a great composer and pianist of the past, and no doubt also for the prodigious talent and mastery of the great Paderewski; but she was not humble before their presence, daring to play on the piano that once was played by Beethoven himself, and expecting Paderewski to do the same.

In the other sense of being good, being accomplished at what we do, our work, a sport or hobby, we thrive on the admiration of others. We like to show off our talents, often at the expense of those less gifted. In this sense too, being good is not good enough. We must know the limitations, pettiness, and emptiness of our being. We must become humble in all that we think, all that we speak, all that we do.

If we are truly bowing our heads before the Dhamma, that is itself our liberation. The perfection that we seek in our lives is already there; we need only to be truly humble to achieve it.

Beyond these walls

Don't let your judgment be clouded
by selfish desires
that can obscure loving kindness

It was late on a Friday evening. Arun had been working hard all week and he was tired, mentally and physically. Even at this late hour the traffic on the expressway was still heavy, and now it began to rain. A few heavy splashes at first, that didn't quite seem to need the windscreen wiper. Then suddenly, down it came in a great rush.

Arun turned the wipers on full speed, but even then it was difficult to see ahead and he slowed down, straining his eyes through the dancing torrent to make out the lights of the other vehicles. And then came the thud as his pickup was hit from the rear. He heard the crunch of metal against metal and felt a terrible pressure on his chest, and then all was blackness.

When he next opened his eyes he could see only the white ceiling of the hospital room. His seat belt had saved his life, but he had suffered severe injuries. He was able to speak and hear, and even see, but for many weeks he would be immobilised, unable to turn his head more than a fraction either way.

Soon with the aid of a mirror he was able to take stock of his surroundings and realised the voice that had intro-duced itself as Surapon was that of his roommate, an elderly man who several months before had been crushed by a heavy load in the factory where he worked. He too was quite ill, but as people tend to do in such situations, they soon began to talk to one another whenever possible.

One day Surapon, whose bed was next to the only window in the small room they shared, was able to sit up for the first time. Starved of the signs and sights of the outside world Arun was excited at the new possibility of knowing through his fellow patient something of what was happening beyond their four walls.

With the limited movement of his right hand he was able to adjust the mirror and was able to see Surapon propped up on his pillows. "What can you see, what can you see now?" he demanded excitedly. "I can hear children's voices. What's going on?"

"Oh, there's a beautiful park down there, right next to the hospital. There's a pond. Children are sailing little boats. And there's a dog just jumped in the water after a stick."

"What else, can you see beyond the pond? Come on, please tell me more."

And so it was that every day when Surapon was allowed to sit up he described what he could see through the window. It came to be the high point of their day, and even when Surapon seemed tired Arun kept on at him to find out what was going on outside.

One day as Surapon was being propped up by the nurse, it began to rain. They could hear it pattering at first on the roofs outside, then pounding down with the roar and force of a downpour. Just as suddenly it stopped, and Arun as usual was eager to maintain his connection with what he believed was the real world—his world that had been so cruelly and unfairly wrenched from him. "So what's going on in the park now? Is anybody there?" The nurse had been about to leave, but now she looked quizzically first at Arun, then to Surapon who had twisted his head to the window that was parallel with his bed. She paused for a moment, then walked over to Surapon and straightened his wispy hair gently with her fingers and smiling silently to herself, she quietly left the room.

That day, Surapon described the park as it slowly shook off the rain and once more welcomed the warming rays of the sun. How people began to appear on the still wet paths. How the sun once more danced on the water and children reappeared, playing along the water's edge.

Arun longed to see this all for himself, and knew if he were by the window he could position his mirror for a perfect view; and anyway, perhaps soon he too would be able to sit up.

He thought more and more about this. Why should the old man have the best position? Why should he have to rely on him for a secondhand commentary when he could see for himself if his bed was close to the window?

As the days went by he became more and more resentful and began to lose interest in the daily descriptions from Surapon, who far from improving seemed to be getting weaker, judging from his voice and the long silent periods when he appeared to be asleep.

Just as he had hoped, the doctors told Arun that in a few days he would be able to sit up, and if things went well, they might even be able to remove the brace from his neck that had kept him almost immobile. But, he was warned, there would be weeks, possibly months ahead of being confined to his hospital bed. Having that window position became even more important to Arun, and in his selfish obsession, Surapon became an obstacle to his goal.

That very night he was awakened by the noise of violent coughing. The light was dim but with a practised twist of his mirror he could see Surapon slumped half out of bed, his body jerking with each cough. Arun reached for the button that would summon the nurse and then stopped, letting it slip from his hand as the body of the old man slid almost in slow motion on to the cold tiles of the floor. When Arun finally pressed the call button it was almost dawn, and Surapon's lifeless body was removed as if it were just a bundle of soiled sheets.

It seemed certain now that Arun would get his wish. "Of course we'll move you by the window this afternoon. This morning we'll get you sitting up without your head brace," said the nurse, adding, "I expect you'll miss Surapon, you really came to rely on him, didn't you? You know, he had a very kind heart, as I am sure you will soon realise."

Puzzled slightly by the nurse's last remark Arun occupied himself with the anticipation of his new found freedom, quickly dismissing any thoughts of his former roommate.

Finally, about the same time as when he used to listen to Surapon's halting yet compelling descriptions of the park and all the comings and goings that so enlivened his day, he was wheeled to his coveted position by the window. And now he could even turn his head. The warm afternoon sun had already brightened the window frame and Arun slowly, almost breathlessly, twisted his head to catch the view that Surapon had so often described.

The sign on the grey wall opposite said "Parking" and all around were the bare grey walls of the hospital car park . . .

How often do we allow our judgement to be clouded by selfish desires? Desires that can obscure loving kindness. Desires that can twist our thinking until we become so obsessed with satisfying them that other people are seen merely as an obstacle to be removed.

Desires that eventually will bring us up against a blank wall.

It's never too late

Unacceptable behaviour by others
must not intrude into our inner silence

Two reports in a local newspaper caught my eye. The first was a heartwarming account of how veteran actor Tony Curtis, then 77, was appearing in a stage version of the classic musical *Some Like It Hot* in which he first starred more than 40 years ago.

Why heartwarming? Well, apart from the great photo showing the actor in a reassuringly relaxed and familiar pose which said "If he can do it, so can anyone," the story of his struggle and final success in overcoming both alcohol and drug addiction and his reappearance at this time of his life in an active stage role, all that is extremely heartwarming.

It's also a lesson in the dangers we all face in this increasingly liberal society. Describing how he had succumbed to some of these dangers, Curtis talked of how the breaking point for him came in 1981. "I wasn't happy with my marriages, I wasn't happy with the films I was getting. The next thing I know, I'm using cocaine and alcohol, and the next thing I know, I'm immersed in it." It's a familiar story, especially for those showered with fame and fortune. In the case of this particular star he recognised the danger and did something about it.

The other report was about another actor, Kevin Kline. The essence of the story was how the actor seemed to identify with a character he played in his then latest film, an old-fashioned prep-school professor.

A key point in the film illustrated how the highly principled teacher in a battle of wills with a rebellious student finally gave in to human frailty and bent his own principles. Commenting on this, Kline, who was highly praised for his portrayal of the teacher, said, "Hundert (the teacher) doesn't live up to his own principles. He gives in to human frailty. I think we can all relate to that. What he eventually sees is the seduction of our culture by the well packaged person or idea."

And referring to the student named Sedgewick he added, "It's the prevalent rationalisation that the end justifies the means. That's what drives Sedgewick—he wants to win, and he doesn't care what it takes."

That last comment gave me much pause for thought. It seemed to highlight much of what causes disharmony in our society today. A craving for success or recognition of one kind or another, a lack of loving kindness, intolerance, dishonesty, and a complete lack of humility.

Speaking of what he saw of the attitude of youngsters today, the actor said, "A lot of kids just want to work as little as possible, and make the most possible money. There's no love of learning, of acquiring knowledge and wisdom, of understanding history or current events. They don't know what's going on in the world. They want to kick back and play with their computers and watch TV."

Kevin Kline was no doubt referring to American children, but he could well have been talking about youngsters in most countries around the world. Certainly many Thai parents could identity with his sentiments.

In the competitive world of business, this behaviour is all too common. We meet it in the work environment, often almost daily. We may wonder sometimes what we're doing wrong.

The rudeness, arrogance, or plain mean-minded attitude of a colleague or boss can have a devastating effect on everybody around them. They seem to be intent only on achieving their own ambitions, not caring who they trample on in the process.

So, how do we deal with this kind of problem, of the behaviour of those who want to win and don't care what it takes? This survival of the fittest philosophy now being made even more fashionable by programmes that seem to glorify winning at any cost?

First we must recognise that it is the problem of the individual who behaves that way. Unacceptable behaviour by others of any kind is just that. It should not, and must not, intrude into our inner silence. It must not cause even a ripple on the surface of our pool of calmness and serenity. It only exists if we admit it.

We can also see that to thrive, bad behaviour to others requires an audience, a target for its barbs, sneers and putdowns. We must also remember that people who are consistently unpleasant to others are often battling their own fears and demons. Others will justify their actions by claiming they can't afford to show weakness by being kind or considerate to others. They live in fear of themselves.

A little girl, constantly rejected by her father when she tried to climb on his lap for much needed affection, finally asked her mother tearfully, "Mummy, why does Daddy hate me so much?" Taking the child in her arms, the mother explained, "He doesn't hate you, dear, he's just scared of loving you."

There were many lessons in those two articles, with the comments of Kevin Kline reminding us that the end-justifies-the-means mentality is also reflected in politics and business. But it was the image of 77-year-old Tony Curtis, smiling broadly, that reminded me so graphically that by looking within ourselves, we can find happiness and contentment.

Changing times

**The natural inclination to cling
to the past is a road to nowhere**

"The party's over, it's time to wake up." Those half remembered lines of a once popular song take on a new meaning as we look forward, perhaps with some uncertainty and even trepidation, to yet another New Year. Another? Well, New Years do have a habit of coming around with monotonous regularity. And in spite of all the revelry that marks the annual passing of the old and the advent of the new, their very persistence can be an unwelcome reminder of the relentless passage of time.

As we get older our perspectives inevitbly change, and as such New Year comes and goes we have to make adjustments. The cosy world of our youth no longer exists. Familiar icons, stars of the entertainment world for instance, have been growing old like the rest of us, but we haven't given it much thought; and when suddenly we see them as they are today, well, it can be quite a shock. Sometimes if the person was a special favourite of ours we feel somehow let down. "How can anybody change so much? I can't believe it's the same person," we say when perhaps we see one of our favourite stars in a television interview. We tend to forget of course that we too have changed. And when we're confronted head on with that most unwelcome of facts, we are most reluctant to accept it.

Have you ever looked at contemporary photographs of yourself and felt almost embarrassed at how unattractive and old you look? Years later you come across those same photographs and just can't help almost saying out loud, "Wow, is that me? I can't believe I looked so young. I looked great." Friends who are shown the photos tend, of course, to put us in our place with comments such as, "Yes, so what happened?"

It does seem to be a well known trait of human nature that however much we may be aware of the impermanence of all things, of the cycle of birth, life and inevitable death, we desperately want to believe that as an individual we are different. As adolescents, perhaps after a visit to our grandparents, we might well have said, "I'm never going to be old. I couldn't bear to look like that."

The Buddha reminded us of the five fundamental truths of existence that cannot be challenged and apply to every one of us:

1. Growing old is a natural condition. There is no way to escape it.
2. Suffering ill-health is a natural condition. There is no way to escape it.
3. Death is a natural condition. There is no way to escape death.
4. Everything and everyone changes; we must part even from loved ones.
5. My thoughts and my actions are my only true belongings. I cannot escape the consequences of my actions. My actions are the ground on which I stand.

Just as there is no escape from these fundamental truths, there is also no escape from the absolute necessity of their acceptance. Growing old can be described as the Dhamma of all composite things. And when we fully accept that eternal truth, our fears of growing old, of becoming ill, of losing loved ones, and of our inevitable death, will no longer lead us in futile attempts to change the nature of things.

Recently, I watched with a kind of bemused fascination a television programme illustrating the extreme lengths many people, especially those in the entertainment business, will go to in their vain attempts to stay young. Actually when you think about it, the expression "staying young" is both a contradiction and an impossibility.

But that of course does not deter the diehards. They subject themselves to the surgeon's scalpel, to injections of a toxin that effectively paralyses their facial muscles, they endure all manner of abrasive and other treatments and mostly they do it in secret. "My face is my fortune," they say, but they fail to grasp another very basic truth— other people simply don't care. In fact most of us, when confronted by someone who is just too good to be true, will find it makes us uncomfortable and difficult to accept that individual as a person.

For men, perhaps the most common example of age denial are the attempts by the balding to first experiment with every type of remedy and then, when the inevitable happens, to resort to the always obvious toupee. Instead of enhancing the wearer's appearance, the artificial hairpiece is more often a distraction.

This was vividly illustrated in the follow-up to the film classic *The Magnificent Seven* which starred the charismatic and shaven-headed actor Yul Brynner. In the inevitable sequel the original cast was replaced, and Yul Brynner's action role was taken by a middle-aged actor with a hairpiece. Needless to say the film was less than successful, the star being remembered only for his comical appearance.

The natural inclination to cling to the past, though understandable, is literally a road to nowhere. Far, far better then, to follow the wisdom of the Buddha. To accept that we will indeed grow old and that the physical world around us also constantly changes. We can all see dramatic evidence of changes that have taken place in our lifetime, both in the world at large and in the world we have touched and which has been part of our environment.

Think back just a few years, for instance, to a Bangkok without highrise buildings, with no shopping malls or entertainment complexes. To a world without television, without computers and the all-pervasive Internet.

It has been said that the only constant of change is change itself. It might also be said that for many of us accepting change, growing old gracefully is one of life's greatest challenges. The freedom we achieve by overcoming our reluctance to aging can also be one of its greatest joys.

Defeating depression

The despair we feel at destructive events in
the world around us can be cleansing

"How are you today?"
"Actually I'm feeling a bit depressed. I don't know why,
really. Everything seems so pointless. It all seems to be
a waste of time, and I seem to have no energy for anything." At some point we will all have heard a similar
answer. We may well have given such an answer ourselves, instead of responding with the expected "I'm
fine, thanks."

However resolute and positive we are, one day we
wake up to a world that seems overwhelmingly depressing. International conflicts and natural disasters compete

for our attention with a host of unending tales of local corruption and its consequences. Everywhere man's inhumanity to man is reported, often in horrifying detail.

We see and read many reports of the changing weather patterns triggered by our unrelenting pollution of the environment. Of flooding caused by deforestation, wildlife threatened with extinction, natural resources overexploited for short term gain. Enough examples, we say, to fill a book. Indeed many have been written that highlight these dangers, and what appears to be a whole Green industry has sprouted over recent years, dedicated to countering these destructive and polluting forces.

Isn't all this enough to make anyone feel depressed? After all, if what we perceive as the state of the world did not affect us, what would that say for us as individuals?

Being depressed, though, is different from suffering from what nowadays is described as depression—a condition recognised by doctors, yet still not fully understood by psychiatrists. Depression, clinically defined, is a state of extreme unhappiness, described by some sufferers as a black, dismal, dungeon of despair; as a stifling hot room with no means of escape; as a heavy overcoat of pain, or like walking through treacle.

Depression can be precipated by many factors, but from the Buddhist perspective its main cause can be expressed in one word: selfishness. Satisfying our own needs and pleasures above those of everyone else. The "me first" attitude, whether it's pushing to the front of the queue, making sure we get the best food first, the best seat at the show, the most praise for something we do in competition with others.

"Wait a minute," you say, "being selfish may not be a good thing, but how can it lead to depression?" There are two main reasons. First, unhappiness arising from selfishness is cumulative. When we don't get what we want, or are stopped from doing what we want, we often overreact to a ridiculous extent. How many arguments at home or at work have arisen from quite petty causes related to being selfish? Such behaviour naturally isolates us from others, and as this pattern of behaviour is repeated, our self-confidence is eroded.

Self-obsession smothers consideration for the needs of others, and we stop giving love. Our preoccupation with satisfying our own desire to be happy blinds us to the needs of our family and friends, and we do nothing to help them. And because we no longer receive their love in return, or the simple, pure joy of making them happy, the cycle of isolation continues. We sink further into unhappiness, self-doubt, and even thoughts that we are going insane. This is depression.

What can we do to break this depression cycle? First we must recognise that the despair and despondency we feel as a reaction to the negative and destructive events in the world, can in itself be a cleansing act. In the practice of Dhamma we will encounter negative karma as we face up to the suffering we must all experience in this world. When we wash a dirty piece of cloth, for instance, the water becomes black. We don't see the black dirt as a negative thing, since it means the cloth is getting clean. So, in this sense, when we get depressed at this level, we should perhaps rejoice.

To tackle what the medical world calls clinical depression, we clearly need to look deep within ourselves to rid ourselves of the concept of "I". Think about it; without the ego to nourish it, depression cannot exist.

We can also help ourselves in very practical ways. Every morning when we wake up, we have a new day ahead of us. How we make use of that precious time is entirely up to us. Start the day with a smile? Why not, even if it's just laughing at that bleary-eyed image in the bathroom mirror. A friend of mine says each morning as he's brushing his teeth he tries to recall an amusing incident or story from the day before. When he starts laughing he knows it's time for his shower. Apparently his early morning laughter routine is infectious, and when he comes down for breakfast the rest of his family demand to be let in on the joke.

That's the great thing about a cheerful disposition, and its close companion, a sense of humour: they're catching, and there are very few places or occasions where they're out of place. Most public speakers are well aware of the value of humour in putting their audience at ease, and some are wise enough to use it as a means to bring cheer and comfort to others.

My own high point of accidental humour came when as a student I was asked to repeat that well known remark of Britain's Queen Victoria, "We are not amused." I knew it was something to do with humour, but I just couldn't remember the exact words. Finally I thought I'd got it. "Don't make me laugh," I said triumphantly. And since then, I can never think of that period of British history without laughing.

Taking care of number one

We are often so wrapped up
with our own agenda
that we lose sight
of the needs of others

When we refer to people as being selfish, we probably mean they put their own interests first. They force their way aggressively and defiantly on to the skytrain before passengers get off, or demand the attention of the shop assistant even though other people are waiting patiently to be served. Most of us see such behaviour daily and perhaps simply put it down to the decline in social values and the pressures of modern living.

To some of us, though, it's a wake-up call, and we begin to examine our own behaviour. Are we also selfish, putting our own interests above all else, often to the detriment of others? Do we in fact follow the "Me First" philosophy? Before we try to determine the level and nature of our own selfishness, let's take a look at this most basic of human characteristics.

"Chiefly concerned with one's own interest often to the total exclusion of the interests of others." That stark definition of selfishness we find in the dictionary reminds us that there's more to this behaviour than simply being miserly or greedy. Self assertive and selfish behaviour, can, for instance, cause real inconvenience and even hardship to others.

Imagine a long queue of poor people waiting to take advantage of a special offer of children's clothing at a bargain price. For one woman in the queue, this is an important chance to get some badly needed clothes for her three children, who because they can't be left unattended have had to wait with their mother.

As she finally gets near the counter and is about to make her selection, a well dressed, bossy woman suddenly appears from nowhere, brushes the first woman aside and gathers up a wide selection of different items from the display. Nothing suitable is left for the woman who had waited so long, and she has no choice but to leave empty-handed.

If we think about it, we will realise that although selfish behaviour is not always as obvious as this example, it can affect our lives in many ways. The streets and sidewalks or pavements, and now the skytrain walkways of our capital city, are deluged with people and small businesses promoting their activities with little heed to the interests, comfort or even safety of others.

I once had a dinner appointment in the Silom area and decided to walk the last part of the journey to the restaurant, just to see how the construction of the new subway facilities at the intersection was coming along. I jumped out of the car when it stopped at the traffic lights opposite Chulalongkorn Hospital and feeling in a relaxed mood, waited to cross the road with a crowd of other people. The pavement behind me at that spot occupies a wide curve almost in front of the hospital, but still there was not much room for people to walk. The whole area was awash with vendors' carts on one side, and spread everywhere on the other side were displays of souvenirs and various other items.

Following the dictum of safety in numbers, I joined the crowd as we scurried like frightened rabbits across the gauntlet of revving motorcycle and *tuktuk* engines to reach the relative safety of the narrow traffic island in the middle. Another wait, and then a great rush for the other pavement before the vehicles from the Lumpini side roared impatiently around the corner.

Right on the corner two taxis had stopped abreast, while some more crept, vulture-like, beside the kerb. Funneled into an almost impossibly narrow space between the eye-level jutting steel supports of a new footbridge and yet another strategically placed vendor's stall, I struggled to find a way out. Finally, I made it to the kerbside and eyed the waiting traffic warily before I risked another scurry to the narrow centre strip to join a new group waiting to make the Great Crossing. We waited and waited, and were about to surge across that final 20 metres or so when a bus thundered on us, deterring even the bravest. No surprise then, when the lull eventually came, that our small crowd now united by a sort of common despair, almost ran to the other side.

I was hesitant to discuss my Silom adventure with my dinner guests, not wanting to make an issue out of something many people take for granted. But, when finally I commented on the difficulty of simply crossing the road, it appeared that I had touched on a raw nerve. My guests immediately launched into other examples, and soon we were all involved in a lively discussion about how our society has deteriorated; how traditional values have been eroded, how politeness, consideration and courtesy have given way to bad manners, aggression and selfishness, how self-interest increasingly seems to dictate people's behaviour.

It was all rather depressing, and finally one person around the table said, "Hey, we're not here to change the world. What can we do about it, anyway?" Before anyone could reply, he shrugged and smiled, adding, "Besides, we're here to discuss business. We have to take care of our own interests, don't we?"

That well-intended comment, designed to lessen the seriousness of the conversation, in fact pointed to a basic truth. Because we all have our own agendas, the vendors with their sometimes desperate need to make a living, the taxi drivers struggling to compete for fares, the office and shop workers thinking only of getting home after a long day; because of what we perceive as the necessity to achieve whatever goals we have set for ourselves, we subsequently lose sight of the needs of others.

So is this inevitable? Do we simply accept that we're not here to change the world? Yes, people do seem to be more selfish at one level, but perhaps this has always been so. The good news is that there are also countless examples of unselfish behaviour, of people demonstrating loving kindness, compassion and consideration for others.

If we each follow the Dhamma path of unselfishness in every aspect of our daily lives, we can indeed change the world.

Special relativity

Dhamma vision brings true understanding
and perspective on the world

It was a hot afternoon and the
sprurting jets of the water sprinkler were arcing across a
thirsty patch of grass in the garden.

A black and white finch hopped in and out of the free
shower as a cat watched from the shade, too lazy to follow
its instincts and chase after the bird. But a squirrel high
up in the dark, grey-green folds of the mango tree was
as agile as ever. One moment it was poised on a branch,
highlighted by a shaft of sunlight, the next it was gone,
startled perhaps by my incautious approach. From branch

to branch, tree to tree—then in one mighty leap, to the eaves of the house.

I settled down on a seat in the shade thinking about how I fitted into all this. I looked around, took note of the overwhelming presence of green, and then marvelled at the many different shades of that most basic of nature's colours: the light, almost translucent yellowish-green of the banana fronds, the olive green of the leaves of the mature mango tree, and the myriad variegated greens of the plants and shrubbery, all set against the backdrop of the green of the grass.

I watched as an ant crawled over the back of my hand, realising that the indentations on my skin and the ridges created by my veins would from the ant's perspective seem like part of a rather barren landscape. Was that tiny creature aware, I wondered, that it was scurrying over part of another living and breathing creature, albeit of some-what larger proportions? In fact, do ants and similar small creatures have any real sense that we humans exist?

The little bird, perhaps refreshed, had flown off in a sudden swift flight to a high point on a neighbouring house, and the cat, stirred by this departure, stretched and padded off in search of new distractions. I was left

with my thoughts and the ant, which by now was nego-
tiating the patterned holes in the white top of the cast-
iron garden table.

So, how do we humans fit into the world of the bird,
the squirrel, the cat, and the ant? Probably, from their
point of view, just as part of the landscape. Each of them
lives in a different universe of sizes and shapes, sounds,
sights and smells. The small finch enjoying its garden
shower has a lifespan of from perhaps five to 15 years;
its hearing is much more acute than ours; it sees in colour
and can see ultra-violet light—oh yes, and it can fly.

The "garden" squirrel can't fly but it can move faster
in a tree than it can on the ground, and can fall around 30
metres without getting hurt—it uses its tail as a sort of
parachute. It probably only sees in black and white, and
has a lifespan similar to that of the finch with which it
shares its territory.

And the ant? We're told it lives on average about five
years, but it's difficult to imagine how the world must
appear to this tiny insect. Although it sees in colour, it
appears to hear and communicate very selectively using
a kind of vibration system. This means when it's trapped
underground it can send out a message to the Ant

Rescue Service, but is oblivious to the noise generated by humans. So no use shouting at it to go away, better to learn ant talk.

I had been sitting there for quite some time, musing about the different worlds and dimensions occupied by the creatures I had seen. The light now was beginning to change. Soon it would be that dreamtime so beloved by photographers; soft mellow tones, slowly fading hues as the day wound down. Whose world is it anyway? Isn't it yours and mine? After all, what would an ant know about photography, or the finch and the squirrel for that matter?

The answer is that the world as we experience it belongs to the moment, whether seen through the sharp eyes of a bird, the black and white vision of a squirrel or the-still-to-be-understood senses of the ant. It's obvious enough that animals, birds, and insects will perceive "our world" differently from one another and from us.

But do we overlook how we too, you and I, also see things differently from one another?

Once, on a trip to a forest with some friends, an older member of our group just stood gazing from our viewpoint at the panorama of the distant hills and the forest canopy below. We all paused, wondering what had caught his eye. All we could see were a mass of treetops and the vague shapes of the faraway hills. "I used to come here as a kid," he said. "Over there, there used to be a stream. The water was so fresh you could drink it." We smiled and nodded, understanding a little more about our own perceptions of the world in which we are just fleeting visitors.

Accepting that every one of us experiences the world differently, allows us to truly understand the feelings and sensitivities of others. But to do this takes more than just a sort of passive acknowledgement that we are indeed all different. We must make that extra effort to see the world through the eyes of all those we come in contact with. We must practise a special kind of empathy; we must see and listen to the world through Dhamma Vision and Dhamma Hearing. With the understanding and insight that comes from Dhamma wisdom also comes compassion and loving kindness.

Before I left the garden, a truly magnificent butterfly fluttered onto a nearby flowering shrub. Yet another view of the world. How long, I wondered, does a butterfly live? I looked it up. On average, about one month. To the butter-fly, a lifetime. To you and me, a few chance encounters in the garden.

The perils of procrastination

**Life's problems, once tackled head-on
and with determination, can be overcome**

Procrastination, the old say-ing goes, is the thief of time, and it's something of which we are all guilty. It's also been described as "The Art of Keeping Up with Yesterday."

We venture into the spare room to look for something we stowed away months ago and say to ourselves, "I'll have to clean this mess up soon." Then we shut the door, literally and symbolically, hiding it from our eyes. We may even resolve to tackle it the next day, but of course, then there will be another excuse. Procrastination never lets up. The friend of laziness, it promotes guilt and a feeling of resentment at our own weakness.

Having an untidy spare room may seem trivial in the scheme of things, but it's symbolic of the problems procrastination can bring, especially in our approach to work. Whatever we do for a living there is always a multitude of tasks, some more challenging than others that need to be tackled. Putting off until another time what can and should be done right away, can also create a multitude of troubles. We all know that today's minor task left undone becomes tomorrow's major problem. The report that should be finished today, those appointments that must be made for the visiting executives.

So why do we procrastinate? Is it just laziness, a kind of torpor that we find difficult to shake off? Or is it simply a lack of motivation? If, for instance, we knew that important guests were on their way to stay with us, that spare room would surely be cleaned up in no time. And if we knew that by completing our tasks at work in a timely fashion we would be in line for an important promotion, wouldn't we redouble our efforts to catch up with all our outstanding tasks, even doing some things ahead of time?

For many of us our student days shape our attitudes to life. These are times when procrastination rules or is seen as a challenge to be overcome. In my case, I had been studying hard for weeks, working into the night, doing my best, as I thought, to prepare myself for the coming exams. Some nights I would simply fall asleep with a book in my hands and wake up the next morning still dressed in yesterday's clothes. After a shower, a snacked breakfast from the fridge, and a change of clothes I would resume my cycle of reading, researching, eating and occasionally falling asleep.

From time to time, I would gaze around my apartment which had deteriorated into an untidy mess and resolve yet again to do something about it "as soon as I have time." Finally, one bleary-eyed evening I ran out of food and had to venture out to the 24-hour supermarket round the corner. As well as food and essentials, I had the foresight to buy a pack of large black garbage bags, thinking they would come in useful later.

Laden with my shopping I was struggling to get the key into the door of my small apartment when I noticed a strange unpleasant smell. By the time I had managed to juggle the bags of shopping and open the door, I realised much to my embarrassment, that the smell was coming from my own kitchen. The overflowing waste bin, the dishes crammed into the sink, the pile of unwashed laundry. . . Procrastination had caught up with me in a big way and I liked it not one bit.

Not liking it is one thing, but doing something about it, especially at that hour when all I wanted to do was to fill my stomach and sleep, was a challenge and I thought I was about to fail. I had found a place to dump the shopping and looked around, assessing what I would have to do in the Big Clean up. Tomorrow, it will have to be tomorrow, I thought, feeling I simply had no energy to tackle it there and then. Procrastination looked as if it was about to steal another chunk out of my life. Just then, though, I made a great decision. Before I go to bed, I said to myself, I'll do all the dishes, clean the fridge and put the shopping away. At least I'll have made a start; the rest of the cleaning I would do the next day.

Yes, you've probably guessed what happened. Once I'd got into the swing of things I simply carried on until the Big Clean up became Mission Completed. I even discovered a textbook I had been convinced must have self-destructed but which somehow reappeared in the laundry basket; living in an untidy mess can result in some strange things.

My big lesson from that early encounter with my own procrastination was that like so many of life's problems, once tackled head on and with determination, it can be overcome. And the rewards are many. There is of course the immediate and practical benefit of simply getting the job done. There's the sense of satisfaction of having risen successfully to the challenge. There's also a new clarity of mind, free from the nagging distractions of things yet to be done, a clarity that inspires you to stay ahead of the procrastination game.

In my case, working in a clean and orderly environment made my studying very much easier. I planned my schedule, including time out for exercise and relaxation and daily chores around the apartment. This meant cleaning up after every meal, doing the laundry on a regular basis, not staying up too late, and getting up early.

Most of the jobs we put off doing tend to be those we regard as unpleasant and time-consuming. To escape from the relentless pressure of procrastination we must approach every task in a mindful and humble fashion, aware of the moment.

Whether doing our daily chores, checking and replying to our email, getting that report done on time, everything we do deserves our full attention. When we provide that, the completion of each task will have its own reward.

Naturally, not everything can be given top priority, but by applying a planned and systematic approach to the jobs that will always lie ahead, we will banish procrastination from our lives and become skilled practitioners of that other art, "The Art of Keeping Up with Tomorrow."

Empty words

Don't make promises
if you can't keep them

"OK, I promise I'll have it done by the weekend." "Are you sure?" "Yes, I'm sure—don't worry, I promise." Making promises is something we all do. More often than not, we also break them. Children quickly learn the value of those two words, "I promise." They seem to offer a perfect way to turn off the flow of parental nagging. "Please, Mom, all my friends are going. I won't be on my own. You don't have to worry, I promise I'll come straight home as soon as the concert's over."

In turn, parents will use the promise to control their children. "OK, you two, I need you to be on your best behaviour when our visitors arrive. If you show what really good children you can be, then I promise there'll be a trip to the seaside at the weekend. Plus I promise to ask your father for that pocket money rise."

We make promises to others and to ourselves. "I've always promised myself that one day I'll take a trip to Europe. . ." Often those kinds of promises remain unfulfilled, but they serve to spur us on. To work harder at whatever we're doing so that one day we'll be free to pursue our dreams. We tell ourselves that everyone needs a dream, remembering perhaps the words of that song from the musical *South Pacific*:

"You gotta have a dream,
If you don't have a dream.
How you gonna make your dream come true?"

Daydreams, vague ambitions that one day we'll make our mark, earn the respect of others, especially that of our peers, by some great achievement so we can bask in the glory of recognition, these surely are harmless promises to ourselves. Don't they help us cope with the business of getting through another day? After all, we say, for some people dreams do come true. We often hear of individuals who have achieved a long-held ambition and who seem to revel in what they're doing. "This is something I've always wanted to do. I feel I'm the luckiest person alive. I love my work and I'm actually getting paid for it," they say.

But realising those dreams, making those self-promises come true, demands a little more than just wishful thinking. Yes, we need to think out a strategy, we must have a plan, but if we are to succeed it must be a plan of action. Along the way we can dream a little, look ahead to when we too can say, "This is what I've always wanted to do." But we have to make it happen.

A cynical view of promises is that they are the stock-in-trade of politicians and the currency of people who owe us money. In fact a promise to pay is the very foundation of trade and commerce. There is, for example, the Promissory Note—a document which promises to pay a given sum to a stated payee on a certain date. In some cultures promises are undertaken on behalf of others, and sometimes, no doubt, against their will. A young woman is promised as a bride by her parents; she in turn may have to promise to do their bidding to keep them free of debt.

Less cynically, young romantics will pledge their undying love, promising to remain ever faithful to one another.

In fiction at least, dying heroes extract promises from those comforting them. "Promise you'll take care of my young Beth, promise me now."

More cynics will say that promises are made to be broken—mere devices to buy time, to win someone's favour, to tempt them with that promise of a lifetime, an offer too good to refuse. The implication being, of course, that people foolish or gullible enough to believe such empty promises deserve what they get, or rather don't get. The very notion of being promised something extravagant by others can cause us to be instantly suspicious of their motives. What are they really up to, we wonder. Why are they promising so much? Can they really make good on their promises? Why should I trust them anyway? All this doubt and suspicion raised by a simple expression intended to reaffirm our sincerity, our intention to do what we've said we will do.

The cynicism associated with the promise has given rise to several shrewd observations including an old Arab proverb stating that a promise is a cloud; fulfilment is rain. Napoleon Bonaparte advised that the best way to keep one's word is not to give it, and George Chapman, an early English writer, observed that a promise is most given when the least is said.

One area where not keeping promises can have devasting effects is at work. And the word here is: don't. Don't make them if you can't keep them. Breaking promises of meeting deadlines, fulfilling given tasks, even answering emails and returning telephone calls—"I'll call you back within 30 minutes"—can quickly lead to loss of credibility and the trust of colleagues, and perhaps even worse, of employers.

Sometimes we use the promise as a means of self-discipline. We promise to complete a particular task by a certain time, and by making that commitment to others we give ourselves a self-imposed deadline. This seems to be a sensible way to make sure we get things done on time while also encouraging us not to be lazy. But why do we need to promise? Why can't we simply do what we say? There is, after all, a clear distinction between a promise and its fulfilment. Isn't it better if we behave in such a way that people don't need to extract promises from us? That when we commit to a certain course of action, everyone accepts without question that we do indeed mean what we say, that we will do our very best to fulfil that commitment? In other words, that we do and not promise, rather than promise and not do.

When we think about it, those two words, "I promise," will be completely unnecessary when we simply follow the basic Dhamma wisdom of applying Right Thinking, Right Speaking, and Right Action.

A life of non-stop surprises

**Keeping a firm grip on the present is essential
if we are truly to accept our place in time**

At whatever age we are, we
are always young or old relatively speaking. A three- or
four-year-old toddler will refer to his year-old sibling as his
"baby sister". His seven-year-old brother will be his big
brother, and to the 11-year-old, they're his "kid brothers
and sisters". Mom and Dad will talk of them as being their
"kids" or perhaps, less derogatorily, their children.

As we progress through life this ingrained habit of
thinking of others as being either younger or older than
ourselves persists. School friends, colleagues at work,

family members and friends, social acquaintances, even public figures and entertainment personalities, they all have their place in our mental age-related filing system.

We also use this method to create a sort of moving private universe where everybody and everything with which they are associated are all relative in the sense of the time and space they occupy, both to one another and to ourselves. As we get older, this leads to our developing a sort of Peter Pan view of the world. Our favourite nephew will always be that fresh-faced youngster who seemed to be permanently attached to a skateboard, and our best-loved singer will be equally ageless in our private and timeless world. This skewed scheme of things can lead to more than a few surprises, even shock.

Just recently, I heard the sound of what today probably qualifies as a "Golden Oldie" from the television in another room. It was one of my favourites and one which I always associated with the American singer Andy Williams—incidentally, I'm not that old! There he was in what looked liked a modern production—one of those music videos. He was seemingly waltzing with a lithe, young and very contemporary beauty. Wow, I thought. He hasn't aged a bit. What's his secret?

Then the scene changed. There was the same young woman and that unforgettable voice of Andy Williams, but this time it seemed to be coming from a white-haired granddad. I stared unbelievingly; surely, that couldn't be. But those features, although now crowned by thinning white hair, were completely unmistakable. It was indeed that veteran vocalist, Andy Williams himself. I was shocked, so shocked in fact that I hurried back to my study to look him up. According to the entry in my *Book of Favourite Songsters*, the crooner was born in 1930! Good old Andy—and silly old me.

The "silly old me" syndrome can give us all sorts of surprises. We look with amazement, for instance, at the grasp of computer and IT skills demonstrated by some of today's even very young children. Recently I witnessed a father struggling to do something apparently challenging with his mobile phone. I was close enough to hear his sighs of exasperation. Finally, his son, who looked no more than six or seven said, "Give it to me, Dad." Within seconds and within one hand still holding a half-licked ice cream, he had done whatever was necessary and handed the phone back to his father. Perhaps the father of this pint-sized prodigy was no longer surprised, but I was.

I was so taken aback by the episode that I recounted it later to friends over dinner. Another surprise: none of them was impressed. In fact, they showered me with similar stories of their own. I was humbled, and they were surprised by my apparent unawareness of what they said is the reality of our times. I kept quiet for the rest of the evening, but I must admit I now view even the very young generation with a new-found respect!

Because we're all guilty of the self-deception that comes from our apparent need to keep the past alive, we must be aware of its dangers. But surely it's harmless enough, we say. Isn't it better, for instance, to remember a loved one or even a favourite singer when they were at their best? Fond memories are one thing, but a craving for a world and a time which no longer exist, is both foolish and eventually unrewarding.

Keeping a firm grip on the present is essential if we are truly to accept our place in time. That place, however much we wish we could turn back the pages in the Book of Life, will always be now, the present moment. We must remind ourselves also that the present is possible only because of the certainty of change in the world as we know it. Fully accepting that truth will help us achieve

Dhamma wisdom and the understanding it brings with it. It's a clarity that comes from breathing, thinking, seeing, speaking, acting and literally being in and of the present moment.

Do not dwell in the past, says the Buddha, do not dream of the future, concentrate the mind on the present moment.

Another veteran performer, Hollywood film actor Kirk Douglas, seems to be living in the moment and enjoying it. He has played the grandfather figure in a serialised drama in which most of the actors are members of the Douglas family.

One thing seems for sure: he's likely to hold the attention of the audience whenever his character speaks. In his 80s and recovering from a stroke, which had left him temporarily speechless, he explained that because he has to enunciate very slowly and deliberately he almost always gets everyone's attention. "They think I am about to say something important," he said, very slowly and deliberately. He also said he was still learning.

Surely that's a lesson for all of us.

Stand up to be counted

For some rare individuals
there's never any doubt
about the right course of action

Y ou are strongly opposed to
smoking, and whenever you can, you point out the perils
of puffing on that perilous weed. You may not be so
forthright in your condemnation as King James I of Eng-
land, who in 1604 provided the definitive anti-smoking
tirade, but you constantly point out its evils. King James's
lurid description, "A custom loathsome to the eye, hateful to the nose, harmful to the brain, dangerous to the
lungs, and in the black stinking fumes thereof, nearest
resembling the horrible Stigian smoke of the pit that is
bottomless," may be couched in the English of the times,
but its meaning couldn't be more clear.

So there you are, relaxing over a beer with a group of friends, when one, then another lights up a cigarette. What do you do? Read them the King James riot act? Ask them not to smoke in your presence? Or do you say nothing, trying your best to ignore the stinking fumes until you have to back away from their effects?

This type of situation is one we often encounter, and one that can pose something of a dilemma. If we do protest, we risk upsetting what's meant to be a convivial get-together. If we say nothing we aren't being true to our convictions, plus we're likely to be physically affected by the cigarette smoke. Because you're with friends, you can say something like, "You know how much I dislike smoking, so if you don't mind I'll just get some fresh air for a while. By the way, you can get me another beer while I'm gone." If you don't drink alcohol either, you of course risk being regarded as a bit of a bore, but you won't have offended your friends or compromised your stand on smoking. Also, simply by expressing your views, your message may have some effect. After all, it's their selfish actions that have caused you to react.

Smoking, though, is just one of the problems that confront us in today's turbulent society, and they all challenge us to do what is right. Do we stand up and be counted, as they say, railing against the evils we see around us? Or do we turn our face to the wall and let it all go by? Do we step over the drug addict, sprawled senseless across our path, shy away from the Aids victim, stare in morbid fascination as a road accident unfolds before our eyes, but do nothing to help the blood-splattered victims?

For some rare individuals there is never any doubt about the right course of action. They make it their life's work to help others. Around the world, they achieve a fame they probably do not seek, a fame which also helps them get things done. But what of the rest of us? We may even look upon those champions of the poor, the sick and the underprivileged with a certain amount of envy. They at least have made it clear where they stand, their conscience is clear. What are we to do? Do we walk into a gambling den in Klong Toey and denounce the assembled throng of drug pushers, addicts, pimps and prostitutes as worthless members of society, asking them to mend their wanton ways or else? Do we challenge the endless corruption that we see all around us?

We justify our inaction by asking ourselves what good it would do anyway. If we stop to help every helpless person we come across, we say, we would bring all kinds of trouble on ourselves—having to be responsible for hospital bills for instance, being late for work, and anyway they're usually just drunks who are sleeping it off, we'd be wasting our time trying to help them. Of course we're never really convinced by those arguments, but for many of us that's how it is; a daily dilemma we cannot escape and which we sometimes try to resolve by some act of merit-making or charity work. "I want to do the right thing, but I am just one individual," we say.

If we think back to the issue of smoking, we know of course that this was not a problem in the time of the Buddha, there were no cigarettes around in his time, but he did warn against the use of intoxicating and harmful substances. When we smoke, we not only hurt ourselves, we're also hurting other people.

As far as smoking is concerned, we can make a stand simply by not doing it, and there are countless ways we can actively campaign against it, including through the many existing anti-smoking organisations. And the same goes for all those other evils which confront us.

When we take the hand of an Aids patient who is lying without family or friends in a hospital bed, we are doing more than simply offering comfort. By helping others in this way we are also helping ourselves. Overcoming fear and prejudices and helping those in need can be a potent force in encouraging others to do the same.

I was reminded of this recently when I came across an account of the work at Wat Hua Rin at Tung Satoke, near Chiang Mai, under Abbot Dhannawat who runs a programme to unite local people in the fight against Aids. He explained, "When we started six years ago the problem was on both sides—people who had HIV-Aids were secretive, while the community would not accept them. Everything was negative, threatening the community's ability to survive peacefully. So we set out to teach people about the importance of solidarity, of helping others—not only in relation to HIV-Aids, but as a whole. We started groups for women, for children, for young people, for seniors and for people living with HIV."

Today the Abbot works with the *Sangha Metta* (The Compassionate Society) project run by Unicef as part of its Thailand country programme. Sangha Metta enlists Buddhist monks and nuns, through scripture, in the fight against the disease. The Four Noble Truths—suffering, its cause, its cessation and the path leading to its cessation—underpin the programme. The driving force in the Sangha Metta is Laurie Maund, 56, an Australian Buddhist who has lived in Thailand for 32 years, and is now professor at the Mahamakut Buddhist University (MBU) in Chiang Mai. From there, he manages Sangha Metta for Unicef.

Reading of the inspiring work of Abbot Dhannawat and the Sangha Metta reminded me once again that if we really want to be counted, all we have to do is to stand up.